Acknowledgments

This project was born late in 1998, but the revelation and insight that made this book possible began more than seven years ago. A special thanks to my dedicated and loyal wife, Pat, who has a real servant's heart. Her intellectual and spiritual contribution were invaluable, and without her hard work and long hours of editing and formatting, this book would not have become a reality. I also appreciate her encouragement and support.

Also, a special thank you to Dean Schoonover for his review of the original, unedited manuscript!

Contents

Preface

Y PEOPLE ARE DESTROYED FOR LACK OF KNOWL-
edge" (Hos. 4:6). This is one of the best
known and most frequently quoted pas-
sages in the Book of Hosea. This passage referred to the
children of Israel and their willful ignorance, rejection
of God's law and lack of obedience. But I believe many
New Testament believers also perish or are destroyed
because of disobedience and/or lack of knowledge. The
Bible is clear on that. Some would argue that those
people were never truly born again, for if they had a
real experience, they would not have grown cold, fallen
away and lost their faith in God. That argument might
be true of some but not of everyone.

I believe there are some who are truly born again
and maybe even serve the Lord sincerely, yet for
many reasons they struggle and sometimes fall away
completely. One reason is their lack of knowledge
about who they are as born-again children of God and
the vital role they play in the body of Christ.

We need knowledge of who we really are in Christ.

The enemy of our soul knows that each of us plays an important part in the body of Christ (the church) and will use every tactic and every means at his disposal to discourage and distract us in order to keep us from reaching our full potential.

Never before in history has so much information been made available to us. This is called the Information Age, and we don't have to look very far to find Bibles, books, video and audiotapes, as well as preaching and teaching, on how to have a relationship with God and achieve spiritual growth and maturity. Yet with all these materials and all this teaching available to us, the church is still experiencing many casualties and failures along the way.

During the early 1970s, a great outpouring of the Holy Spirit was spreading like wildfire. It crossed every denominational line and ushered in the Charismatic Movement, which meant the gifts of the Holy Spirit were in operation and evident in those who were born again and who had received the baptism in the Holy Spirit.

There was a fresh plowing in people's hearts. The people responded to the free gift of salvation being offered, and hundreds of thousands of lives were changed by the power of the Holy Spirit. Church growth exploded, many new ministries were birthed, and preaching and teaching had a renewed vigor. I was saved during this period while reading Hal Lindsey's book *The Late Great Planet Earth.* Many were saved through Hal Lindsey's ministry, and many others through the various great ministries of that day, some of which are still reaching the lost and hurting.

During this outpouring in the 1970s churches were popping up everywhere, some of which became known as mega-churches where thousands attended. These churches were truly blessed as people were growing in the Word of God.

But after a few years, something began to happen. Many of these established churches faltered and came apart at the seams. Believers—faithful men and women of God—fell by the wayside, no longer attending church. Pastors were falling into diverse sins, or becoming discouraged and dropping like flies. Attendance in many churches dropped dramatically, no matter what the size of the church had been before. Some ministers who had been admired as role models were now shunned and looked upon as disgraced. Families were following suit, divorce became rampant, and many found themselves back where they started, wallowing in sin. Why?

I believe there were problem areas in people's lives that were either not addressed or that were completely ignored. The spirit man was born again, but the sinful footholds previously allowed in their lives were never removed or confronted. (See Ephesians 4:27.) For some, it was because of complacency or because the cares of the world were more important than the will of God in their lives. Some people think all is well as long as they are not being struck with a lightning bolt! In any event, many areas of our lives can be caught up in snares, traps and pitfalls if we are *not aware of what they are and how to avoid them.* This is the lack of knowledge that I am talking about in this book—the lack of knowledge that can cause us to perish.

I, too, got off on the wrong track for awhile. In 1987 I walked away from a very effective ministry that God had truly anointed, through which thousands of lives were being changed. Instead, I chose to pursue a secular interest. But God had other ideas. He had a lot invested in me and was not willing to lose out to my personal pursuits, no matter how honorable they were. For three years I was doing my own thing, and in 1990 God used extraordinary measures to turn my life around and put me back on track.

It wasn't that what I was doing was necessarily wrong: it just wasn't what God had planned for me. I wasn't "seeking first the kingdom of God and His righteousness [will]." It seemed that my life was out of control, and it was—for awhile! God had prepared a road that I was required to travel—one of discipline, obedience, dying to self and *complete* trust in Him. That road had room for two, and, indeed, the Lord and I did walk together, hand in hand. I never wavered, never looked back, always pressed forward as God was preparing the way before me, equipping me for a special call to His glory.

This call to ministry was one I would never have chosen, but God had different ideas for me! So, in 1990, the instruction began. His Word was opened up to me like never before. I had a strong desire to see people saved and to see people healed and delivered from all their strongholds as well. This training gave me a much broader understanding of the fuller meaning of salvation. My eyes were opened to the fact that any and all of us as Christians can live under so much bondage and so many strongholds that we *never* have the freedom to truly walk a victorious life, let alone help others!

Tearing down strongholds and breaking generational curses was what God was calling me to do. Jesus came to set the captives free and He opened the prison doors. All we have to do is get up, take what He has freely given, and walk out into complete freedom and liberty. My desire is to show God's people how to do that—how to take God's Word to a higher level in their hearts and in their lives. John 8:36 declares: "Therefore if the Son makes you free, you shall be *free indeed.*"

To God be the glory!

> The Spirit of the Lord God is upon Me,
> Because the Lord has anointed Me
> To preach good tidings to the poor;
> He has sent Me to heal the brokenhearted,
> To proclaim liberty to the captives,
> And the opening of the prison to those who are
>   bound;
> To proclaim the acceptable year of the Lord . . .
>   —ISAIAH 61:1–2

>   —BROTHER VITO
>   HIS BONDSERVANT

Introduction

HIS BOOK WAS WRITTEN AS A LABOR OF LOVE TO inform the reader of the dangerous snares, traps, and pitfalls that plague millions of people around the world! I encourage everyone to take the time to carefully and prayerfully read this entire book because it gives the solution to many of the reasons why born-again believers are not living a victorious life, full of righteousness, peace and joy! I am not offering a quick fix to any and all physical, mental, emotional, spiritual and financial problems because there are many reasons why people have problems. What I will give you in this book are precise strategies for coming out from under any curse or stronghold you may have in your life simply by applying the instructions in God's Word to your situation.

Before I was being prepared for this ministry, when tribulation had come into my own life, I had always looked at it as something that was to be expected as a normal part of my Christian walk. But after a more thorough study of God's Word, I had a better understanding. Jesus said in John 16:33, "These things I have spoken to you, that in Me you may have peace. In the world you will have tribulation; but be of good cheer, *I have overcome the world*" (emphasis added). The apostle Paul says, "Yet in all these things [tribulation, distress, persecution, famine, nakedness, peril, sword (v. 35)] *we are more than conquerors through Him* who loved us" (Rom. 8:37, emphasis added).

This scripture tells us that we are going to have adversity, testing and battles. Without battles, there can be no victories! The real question seems to be, Are we going to lie down in defeat, or are we going to be "conquerors through Him"?

Second Corinthians 10:4–5 declares, "For the weapons of our warfare are not carnal but mighty in God for *pulling down strongholds,* casting down arguments and every high thing that exalts itself against the knowledge of God, bringing every thought into captivity to the obedience of Christ" (emphasis added).

What are the strongholds? I believe they sometimes start innocently enough—maybe with nothing more than a thought. If that thought becomes something we dwell on or entertain for a period of time, then it usually becomes an action or desire of the heart. Once that action is repeated over and over, it becomes a stronghold. Satan is always trying to get a foothold in our lives, and if we allow him in any area of our lives, that action becomes a stronghold. Strongholds always begin as footholds.

James 1:14–15 reads, "But each one is tempted when he is drawn away by his own desires and enticed. Then, when desire has conceived, it gives birth to sin; and sin, when it is full-grown, brings forth death." These footholds may have been allowed to grow and may have been controlling you or your family for many years. A stronghold is any area of your life where you have allowed Satan to seize control and over which you have not gained victory. Strongholds can develop because you may have opened the door through your own sin or disobedience. However, strongholds also can be passed through generational curses—spiritual heredity—through no fault of your own! If we are to experience victory, we must first identify, then root out, pull down and destroy those strongholds.

Not everyone is living under a stronghold of evil. Problems that hinder a person may simply be a fleshly weakness. *You cannot be delivered from the flesh.* The Bible says the flesh wars against the spirit. Whichever one you feed the most will eventually win out! Galatians 5:16 tells us, "Walk in the Spirit, and you shall not fulfill the lust of the flesh." And it goes on to say in verse 24, "And those who are Christ's have crucified the flesh with its passions and desires."

If there is any area in your life that goes beyond the fleshly weaknesses—an area where the enemy has camped out and has established a dwelling place—you can have deliverance, and you can have it by the time you finish this book!

Strongholds Are a Curse

1. They may have originated from past generations.

2. They may come from your own involvement, for example, from transgressing God's law.
3. They may have been spoken into your life.
4. They are a reality and they destroy lives.
5. A curse may either be the result of *your own cooperation,* or it may have been put into motion by someone else, either in your past or present.

If after confession and true repentance,
you are still not free from persistent and uncontrolled
sin habits, then a close examination
of any and all problem areas should be done, and
problem areas should be identified.

Repetition of the same sinful habits may indicate a *deeply-rooted stronghold* in operation. I urge you to ask and allow the Holy Spirit to reveal any and all of the root causes of any strongholds controlling your life.

SPIRITUAL WARFARE

ONE OF THE BASIC PRINCIPLES OF SPIRITUAL WARFARE IS THAT behind most natural circumstances in life there is a spiritual cause. If we are to be successful in waging spiritual warfare, then *we must deal with the root causes rather than surface symptoms.* Just picking bad fruit off a tree doesn't keep more bad fruit from coming back. We must put the spiritual ax to the root! God told the prophet Jeremiah, "See, today I appoint you over nations and kingdoms to uproot and tear down, to destroy and overthrow, to build and to plant" (Jer. 1:10, NIV). Jeremiah, a prophetic intercessor, was instructed to pull down strongholds and to root them out. In other words, he was to put his spiritual ax to the root of evil and terminate its growth for good. God has likewise commissioned us to pull down, root out and destroy strongholds.

Spiritual warfare may be the only remedy for your deliverance. Spiritual warfare is not necessarily easy—no one ever said fighting the devil was going to be easy. You must stand firm! Victory is right in front of you. Claim it; it's yours! As a child of God, we are joint heirs with Christ. Romans 8:17 makes that clear: "Now if we are children, then we are heirs—heirs of God and co-heirs with Christ . . . " (NIV). As an heir, you have a right to claim what is yours. This includes the authority to tear down and remove any and all strongholds from your life so that blessings may be released over every area of your life.

When you put the spiritual ax to the root cause and that root cause is eliminated, growth and reproduction are terminated once and for all. Once you have destroyed the stronghold, you are to "build" and "plant" (Jer. 1:10). This is done by releasing a powerful blessing in your life.

Begin to analyze yourself, your family and your ancestors, if possible. Do you see any signs of a curse or stronghold such as one or more of the following:

1. Repeated failure, constant struggling, feeling defeated
2. Chronic sickness
3. Breakdown of marriage or family relationships

4. Cycle of poverty
5. Mental or emotional problems, depression, etc.
6. Repetitive pattern in the sins of the flesh

Any of these curses or strongholds could have been passed on to you from previous generations as spiritual heredity. It may not be your fault if something was passed down to you from a previous generation, but if you don't want the same stronghold passed down to your children or grandchildren, it is up to you to break it.

You may have already identified some strongholds in your own life or in the lives of your family members. You can renounce the strongholds in your own life, but you cannot get deliverance for someone else. You must reverse the curse and give it back to Satan. *For your authority to be effective, your words should be spoken out loud rather than silently.*

You must bind Satan in the name of Jesus Christ and proclaim to him (Satan) that you renounce that which he put on you and that you no longer accept his control over you or your family. You have the authority in the name of Jesus, and you are exercising your right and hereby taking control of those areas of your life that were under his control. *Do not beg or grovel—stand on faith, not on doubt or unbelief!*

You must be serious in your desire to be set free. The devil will not always lie down on one command, and he might come back again and again from a different direction each time. Don't give up!

You are "more than a conqueror" when you know that you already have the victory before you ever get a problem.

Jesus came to set the captives free. He died on the cross and shed His blood that we might have life and have it more abundantly (John 10:10). It is the appropriated blood of Jesus that breaks any generational curse or stronghold that you may have in your life. May God enlighten you as you apply the holy Word of God (the Bible) in your circumstances, and may you have complete deliverance from bondage by the time you finish this book.

As a child of God, you are not the defeated trying to get victory. If Jesus is in you and you are in Him, you are the overcomer and Satan is trying to rob you of the victory that already belongs to you.

Chapter One

No One Is Exempt!

CURSES—WHAT A STRONG WORD! IT CONJURES UP all kinds of thoughts and horrible conditions, and rightly so! Millions of people live under them, and, more often than not, they do not realize it. The Bible clearly gives us instructions on how to keep from coming under curses! If we transgress God's laws, even after being born again, we will find ourselves struggling with curses. Our own sin is often the open door that allows Satan to operate unhindered in our lives. Do not give him access to your life. The Bible warns us: "Do not give the devil a foothold" (Eph. 4:27, NIV).

If you recognize a curse that is controlling your life, deal with it. The sooner you deal with it, the less entrenched it will become, and the easier it will be to overcome. To deny or ignore the conditions caused by curses can be a major stumbling block preventing victorious living; and many have fallen and not recovered. Clearly, everyone can be subject to a variety of curses of one sort or another. *Born-again Christians are not exempt.*

If you are a born-again Christian and have accepted Jesus as Lord and Savior, you may be asking whether all these curses were broken over your life at the moment of salvation. When you are born again, you are forgiven of your past sins. While it is true that the shed blood of Jesus on Calvary has the power to break any curses in your life, you need to do your part—take authority and break each of them one at a time by the *power of the blood* for the victory to be complete.

For example, physical healing was also provided through the atonement of Christ, yet sickness and disease can still attack us after we are born again.

When that happens, we can receive healing by applying the blood and claiming the healing effected by Christ's atonement, according to Isaiah 53:4–5 and 1 Peter 2:24. In the same way, curses and strongholds can be broken. Everything Jesus purchased for us on Calvary can be obtained by faith—not just salvation and healing!

What Jesus bought for you and I on Calvary includes much more. It includes salvation, healing, the fullness of the Spirit (allowing the Holy Spirit to convict, regenerate, sanctify, anoint, empower, guide, comfort, illuminate your mind, teach and transform you), the fruit of the Spirit (according to Gal. 5:22–23), the gifts of the Spirit (according to 1 Cor. 12:1–11) and victory over the world, the flesh, the devil and all the powers of darkness!

NOW THAT IS SOMETHING TO SHOUT ABOUT!

MAYBE YOU GOT SAVED OR BORN AGAIN, BUT YOU DIDN'T realize that Jesus came and died for you to give you more than a ticket to heaven. He also wants you to have an abundant life here on earth! Many people don't realize everything that has already been done for them and that all they have to do is reach out and accept it—by faith. What a shame! Consequently, they are living "the low life" and settling for it, allowing curses and strongholds to keep one foot nailed to the ground, wondering why "it's always something" in their lives with which they have to deal, never really getting to the real root of the problem.

If you are living under what feels like a curse or a stronghold, make up your mind today that you don't have to settle for less than Jesus provided at the cross!

A curse is a stronghold, and a stronghold is a curse, anyway you look at it—and they can control and destroy individuals, families and nations if we let them. I believe these strongholds of evil are the root cause of our society's ills. The spirit of people has been infected, making day-to-day living more difficult than it needs to be. Not everyone may be dealing with a stronghold, or living under a curse, but almost everyone will have to deal with one or more of them, directly or indirectly, sometime in their lifetime.

We will have spiritual warfare while we are in the

3

flesh. The good news is that God did not leave us defenseless—He gave us weapons! Second Corinthians 10:4 says, "For the weapons of our warfare are not carnal but *mighty in God for pulling down strongholds*" (emphasis added). God has given us the weapons and the authority we need, but strongholds die hard if we are disobedient, self-willed, prideful, fearful or unforgiving.

We must face the truth head-on with the word of truth and learn to use the spiritual weapons found in the Bible.

Even though curses are *spiritual* strongholds, they are manifested in the *physical* realm. From the beginning, God's Word reveals to us how curses have affected the events and circumstances surrounding individuals, families and nations. We read the first recorded account in Genesis 3:14–17 as follows:

> So the Lord God said to the serpent: "Because you have done this, you are cursed more than all cattle, and more than every beast of the field; on your belly you shall go, and you shall eat dust all the days of your life. And I will put enmity between you and the woman and between your seed and her Seed; He shall bruise your head, and you shall bruise His heel."
>
> To the woman He said: "I will greatly multiply your sorrow and your conception; in pain you shall bring forth children; your desire shall be for your husband, and he shall rule over you."
>
> Then to Adam He said, "Because you have heeded the voice of your wife, and have eaten from the tree of which I commanded you, saying 'You shall not eat of it': Cursed is the ground for your sake; in toil you shall eat of it

all the days of your life."

REVERSE THE CURSE!

WE CAN REVERSE CONDITIONS AND CIRCUMSTANCES IN OUR lives that seem to be out of control if we allow the Holy Spirit to transform us. If you know you are under a curse, or suspect you may be, it may not be your fault—it may be a generational curse, which will be discussed in greater detail in a later chapter. It may be the power of negative words over which you have no control that have been spoken against you.

Even though it may not be your fault, it is still your responsibility to take charge of what is going on in your own life and be accountable for your own choices.

Through the power of God, your situation, your circumstances and your destructive habits can be changed. No matter what you may have done, God doesn't want to "get you" for it; He wants to forgive you of it and set you free. The road before us always has a fork in it, because God always gives us a choice! Deuteronomy 30:19 declares that life and death is set before us, and the choice is clearly before us today. If you have made some very wrong choices in your life and you feel your life is more cursed than blessed, it's not too late to get back on the right road and stay there. However, you may have to suffer some consequences from those wrong choices—the Bible clearly tells us we will reap what we sow.

God says that if we will hear and obey His Word we will be successful in *every* area of our lives. He wants to bless us! God backs up His Word, and we can count on it. We must agree and trust God to honor His Word. John 8:36 makes it clear, "Therefore if the Son makes you free, you shall be free indeed."

When all else fails, read the instruction book!

Some of the questions you may have that will be answered in the pages to follow are:

1. What is a curse or stronghold?
2. Where do they come from?
3. Who can be influenced by them?
4. What are the signs that a curse or stronghold is in your life?
5. How do you break through and have complete freedom?
6. How do you keep from coming under a curse or stronghold again?

Are you ready to take charge of your life and be set free? Are you willing to accept change? Changes do not always come with outward appearances.

Any major change in your life requires the renewing of your mind.

May the Holy Spirit enlighten every reader about the dangers that can open the door to strongholds and the devastating effects they can have on one's life. If prayer, confession and repentance were the only things we needed to have complete victory, why are so many Christians still struggling? If you are sincere about living a victorious life and want to break any bondage in your own life, I suggest you pray the following prayer aloud right now:

> Dear heavenly Father, I desire to be set free from any and all strongholds that may be hindering my life. I desire to walk with You and to serve You and to be free of any bondage. I ask You to open my heart and mind to understand the dangers of the snares, traps, and pitfalls, and to give me the wisdom and grace to avoid them. In Jesus' name, I pray. Amen.

Chapter Two

Knowledge
Was the Snare

HE HISTORICAL ACCOUNT OF THE FALL OF MAN IS recorded in Genesis 3:1–19. From the beginning, God blessed all of His creation in Genesis 1 over and over again. Man was not cursed until deception and self-will enticed him to cross the line and he rebelled and disobeyed the one and only command God gave him.

> And the Lord God commanded the man, saying, "Of every tree of the garden you may freely eat; but of the tree of the knowledge of good and evil you shall not eat, for in the day that you eat of it you shall surely die."
>
> —GENESIS 2:16–17

One man and one woman's disobedience created a world of chaos that resulted in the destruction of a corrupt world's society.

> Then the Lord saw that the wickedness of man was great in the earth, and that every intent of

the thoughts of his heart was only evil continually. And the Lord was sorry that He had made man on the earth, and He was grieved in His heart. So the Lord said, "I will destroy man whom I have created from the face of the earth, both man and beast, creeping thing and birds of the air, for I am sorry that I have made them."

—Genesis 6:5–7

The Fall of the Deceiver

The problem didn't start in the Garden of Eden or even on earth. It started long before God created Adam and Eve. The account is recorded by the prophet Isaiah, which refers to none other than the prince of darkness, Satan, the father of lies and deception (Isa. 14:12–14).

This passage points back to the beginning of sin in the universe, when Satan said, "I will." Sin began, and Satan was cursed by his words and by his actions of rebellion.

Spoken Words

God *spoke* the universe, as we know it, into *existence.* He thought it, then spoke it, and it was created. By *words*, everything was blessed, including the serpent in Genesis 3:1. The spoken blessings were interrupted when disobedience was embraced. The serpent referred to in the garden is not to be thought of as a writhing, crawling reptile—that was the effect of the curse upon it for all generations (Gen. 3:14). The

9

creature that lent itself to Satan may well have been the most beautiful as well as the most "cunning" of creatures other than man (Gen. 3:1). Manifested in the serpent, Satan appeared as an angel of light, and, consequently, the following was set into motion:

1. Because the serpent allowed Satan to use him, God *cursed* him, as we see in Genesis 3:14. We curse ourselves and others when we allow Satan to use us.
2. Because of the disobedience of Adam (Gen. 3:17), God *cursed* the ground for Adam's sake. God was saying the ground was cursed, not Adam. However, Adam was formed of the dust of the ground and to dust he would return. While he lived, he would experience pain and hardship—and then he would die. But the real, eternal spirit-man would be redeemed, as God made the sacrifice for him. Adam and Eve were covered by the symbolic blood of Christ when God made tunics of skin, which represented righteousness, to clothe them (Gen. 3:21).
3. The earth would not produce in abundance any longer, as it was under the curse.
4. The earthen vessel would die, though the spirit of man would not.
5. Because man was created in the image of God, he has a conscience and makes moral decisions.
6. Man is the only *creation* that has the ability to speak the spoken word as God does.

Man was created to have dominion over the earth, and has the ability to both bless and curse.

Chapter Three

Spoken Curses

HE SPOKEN CURSE IS DANGEROUS AND MUST NOT be taken lightly, as millions of lives are affected, and many are changed forever by the power of spoken words. There are three categories of spoken curses—to execrate, to vilify and to imprecate. Each of them is expressly forbidden. Each has far-reaching consequences when spoken over someone or something.

1. *Execrate:* To execrate is to call down evil, i.e., wrong, upon someone. It is to condemn them with cutting words, to bitterly denounce, i.e., "You are no good—you will never amount to anything."

2. *Vilify:* Vilification is to defame a person's reputation; to attack them with slanderous and abusive language, especially calling them bad names or talking about or to them using bad names (such as "you stupid idiot"); to speak

fervently and repeatedly in profane terms using profanity or other strong language against someone or thing. This type of curse is put into effect either when one is spoken to or about. Colossians 3:8 tells us to put aside anger, wrath, malice, slander and abusive speech from our mouths.

3. *Imprecate:* To imprecate is the most dangerous curse and more frequently evoked than to execrate. The seriousness and far-reaching effects can be devastating, destroying individuals, families and nations. To imprecate means to evoke (that is, to call or call up) something evil, with the desire of wishing or hoping or expecting something bad to happen to a person, thing or situation.

Example: "I wish that person would get sick or die," or, "I hope that person fails or loses his or her job." A wish or hope with desire can become a negative or positive force put into motion. To damn someone in the same context as wish or hope is to condemn him or her to failure. In other words, a negative wish or hope that is propelled by desire can condemn someone to failure. This is the extreme of spoken curses, and it happens often!

Question: How are we able to condemn by our words?

Answer: In the same way that we can bless with our words!

We are created in the image and likeness of God!

Man is a spiritual being in an earthen vessel and has the power by his or her words to affect the spiritual, as well as the natural, realm.

A curse (or negative, hateful words, or abusive speech) are spiritual condemnations that manifest themselves when spoken in the natural (aloud, out of our mouths).

The word *God* should strike us with awe and reverence, and it does for most people. Yet the word *God* in connection with the word *damn* is used to condemn someone or something to failure. In Exodus 20:7 we read, "You shall not take the name of the Lord your God in vain, for the Lord will not leave him unpunished who takes His name in vain" (NAS). This commandment was given to the children of Israel and to all those who were delivered from Egypt. He said, "I am your God," and if they used His name in vain they would suffer the consequences of punishment. That punishment for disobedience, which they brought upon themselves, would be of an evil nature, leading to all kinds of problems, and it didn't stop with them. That punishment would be passed to future generations (Exod. 20:5). Today we may still be suffering the consequences for our sins in this area, as well as those of our parents and grandparents, if they used the Lord's name in vain (and did not repent of it). If we break this commandment and take the name of the Lord in vain, *we must be quick to repent,* and God will be faithful and just in forgiving us.

What about the non-believer who disregards God's

commandments and frequently uses the word *goddamn* as a byword in his idle conversation, or in anger against another person? The word *profanity* quickly comes to mind! Webster's defines *profanity* as "to treat sacred things with disrespect or contempt." God's commandments are sacred, and when the word *goddamn* is used to curse someone or something, that person is calling upon supernatural powers to condemn that person or thing to an unhappy or very negative fate.

Even if the words are used in a non-condemning way, they are still able to affect a person or thing, causing injury or failure.

The power of the tongue is dangerous and needs to be controlled. To use the evil word *goddamn* is very simply to condemn.

Does the Lord our God condemn someone because an angry person decides to curse him or her? No! God does not condone evil. Then how is that person cursed when someone speaks over them? There is another self-proclaimed god who will gladly see that curses of condemnation will be brought to pass. When we use the name *god* in conjunction with cursing, we evoke/conjure up the powers of evil to condemn—not the powers of the Lord God Almighty. By the spoken words of man, the ruler of darkness, the prince of this world, otherwise known as the god of the world system (Satan), is given access to the cursed person's life to run a course of destruction. This could possibly be health failure, loss of a job, family problems, or even loss of one's life.

Jesus said in John 14:30 that Satan is the ruler of this world.

Satan has the demonic forces to assault us from every direction. When someone evokes the evil he represents, he can send emissaries to inflict all sorts of evil, because he was given permission by man's spoken authority or by our own words or actions.

We must cover ourselves and our families daily, appropriating the power of the blood of Jesus, binding any words or judgments spoken against us, and putting on the full armor of God:

> Finally, my brethren, be strong in the Lord and in the power of His might. Put on the whole armor of God, that you may be able to stand against the wiles of the devil. For we do not wrestle against flesh and blood, but against principalities, against powers, against the rulers of the darkness of this age, against spiritual hosts of wickedness in the heavenly places. Therefore take up the whole armor of God, that you may be able to withstand in the evil day, and having done all, to stand.
>
> Stand therefore, having girded your waist with truth, having put on the *breastplate of righteousness,* and having *shod your feet with the preparation of the gospel of peace;* above all, taking the *shield of faith* with which you will be able to quench all the fiery darts of the wicked one. And take the *helmet of salvation,*

and the *sword of the Spirit,* which is the *word of God; praying always* with all prayer and supplication *in the Spirit,* being watchful to this end with all perseverance and supplication for all the saints.

—EPHESIANS 6:10–18, EMPHASIS ADDED

Chapter Four

Manifestations of a Stronghold

OME STRONGHOLDS MAY BE EASIER TO IDENTIFY by the manner in which they manifest themselves in a person; however, others are more difficult to detect because their manifestations are not as outwardly obvious. The second type is obviously a hidden stronghold. In this chapter I will describe a few of the most common strongholds that are outwardly manifested.

1. Stronghold of anger and rage

Anger is a God-given emotion that we have all experienced at one time or another, and it is not all bad. It's whether we channel it constructively or destructively that makes the difference. Constructive anger can give us the momentum we need to detach from a harmful situation, but uncontrolled anger is another matter altogether. Uncontrolled anger breeds hurtful words, resentments, even violence. Anger and violence go hand in hand, and because of their very nature, are not easily hidden. Proverbs 29:22 says, "An angry man stirs up strife, and a furious man abounds in transgression." Many families are plagued by violence, and many times the one who is out of control does not even realize what he is doing. Consequently, an innocent person often becomes a victim of this stronghold.

In Ephesians we read:

> "When angry, do not sin; do not ever let your wrath (your exasperation, your fury or indignation) last until the sun goes down. Leave no [such] room *or* foothold for the devil [give no opportunity to him]."
>
> —EPHESIANS 4:26–27, AMP

If the devil is allowed to have a "foothold," a stronghold can develop. Ask yourself the following questions:

- Is anger a part of my everyday life?

- Does my anger have an adverse effect on my relationships at home, at work or elsewhere?

- Does my anger flare up easily and often?

- Do I nurse my hurts and cherish my rage?

If the answer was yes to any of the questions above, a stronghold may already be in place.

2. Stronghold of rebellion

Rebellion is another outward manifestation that is easy to identify. Here we are talking about persistent and uncontrolled acts of disobedience towards anyone in authority, including parents, teachers, employers and so on. In 1 Samuel 15:23 we read, "For rebellion is as the sin of witchcraft, and stubbornness is as iniquity and idolatry." Rebellion toward those in authority will cause a person to require an abnormal amount of discipline, and that person will suffer the consequences of his or her rebellious attitude and behavior.

3. Stronghold of pride

Proverbs 13:10 declares, "By pride comes nothing but strife . . . " Strife is connected with pride, and it will manifest contentions wherever it lifts its ugly head. Pride stinks. Proverbs 16:18 says, "Pride goes before destruction, and a haughty spirit before a fall." Pride, haughtiness and arrogance have caused failures in many people's lives. Pride is a destructive force and comes into play when a person has an over-inflated opinion of himself or herself. Pride is the exact opposite of humility, and humility is what pleases God.

4. Stronghold of uncontrolled language

Profanity is like a disease that a person often does not realize he or she has. Cursing is what it used to be called, and rightly so. The person who uses profanity proclaims curses with filthy words spoken about or to someone else. It is abusive language, and the vileness of this stronghold permeates every level of our society. Profanity spews forth from young and old alike, and is, unfortunately, accepted as normal behavior. Today it is unchallenged and allowed in movies, music, print, etc. It has even become commonplace within the family structure and workplace.

These are just a few of the strongholds that are outwardly manifested. Many, many more are hidden (from others, but not from God). Some of the hidden strongholds are adultery/fornication, sexual perversion, pornography, lying and involvement with the occult. Oftentimes, alcohol, drug or gambling addictions are cleverly hidden as well. Many times they are not exposed until lives and relationships are nearly destroyed.

The very fabric of our society is being ripped apart by these strongholds, people want a solution to the problems, but the solution will only come by putting an ax to the root cause of these problems. A Band-Aid simply won't do when surgery is actually what's needed! Why put ambulances at the bottom of the cliff when what we really need to do is build a fence along the edge?

Chapter Five

Bondage Is Slavery!

LAVERY IS A CONDITION THAT MOST PEOPLE FIND repulsive, and rightly so. No one in his or her right mind would want to be a slave! Most countries in the world have abolished slavery as inhumane and degrading. However, some countries still practice slavery in one form or another (without actually calling it that) by oppressive force and control. This causes the governments of free countries to assert pressure for human rights, even, at times, going to war with the oppressor.

When there is a stronghold in a person's life, that person is also being held in slavery. They are in bondage to that habit or circumstance that has them under its control. Webster's dictionary defines *bondage* as "subjection to some force or influence."

Untold millions of people live under conditions of spiritual slavery in one form or another and do not even recognize it as slavery! Romans 6:16, 19–23 makes it clear:

> Don't you know that when you offer yourselves
> to someone to obey him as slaves, you are slaves
> to the one whom you obey—whether you are
> slaves to sin, which leads to death, or to obedi-
> ence, which leads to righteousness? . . .
>
> I put this in human terms because you are
> weak in your natural selves. Just as you used to
> offer the parts of your body in slavery to impurity
> and to ever-increasing wickedness, so now offer
> them in slavery to righteousness leading to holi-
> ness. When you were slaves to sin, you were free
> from the control of righteousness. What benefit
> did you reap at that time from the things you are
> now ashamed of? *Those things result in death!*
> But now that you have been set free from sin and
> have become slaves to God, the benefit you reap
> leads to holiness, and the result is eternal life. For
> the wages of sin is death, but the gift of God is
> eternal life in Christ Jesus our Lord.
>
> —NIV, EMPHASIS ADDED

Slavery to sin, in essence, is bondage, but slavery to
God is eternal life! Many people are held by the grip of
slavery to sin and are resigned to live under it,
accepting it as a way of life over which they seemingly
have no control. Others desire to be free of the bondage
of sin, but they do not know how to be set free.

The Bible describes a stronghold as a spiritual condition that can be pulled down or torn down only by
using spiritual weapons.

> Jesus replied, "I tell you the truth, everyone
> who sins is a slave to sin. Now a slave has no
> permanent place in the family, but a son
> belongs to it forever. So if the Son sets you

free, you will be free indeed."

—JOHN 8:34–36, NIV

There is no doubt that sin, when it is allowed to reign in one's life, controls (enslaves) and holds that person in bondage. There can be one or many strongholds resulting from sin in a person's life, and that person may have tried to break free from the controlling clutches of this particular bondage only to meet with failure time and time again. That person may know exactly what he or she needs to do but is simply unable to do it by his or her own will.

It may be only one sin, a "pet sin," that is gripping a person. That person may deny there is a problem. Perhaps Satan has subtly convinced them that this little pet sin is no big deal to God. Satan always wants us to think our sin is justifiable, and, if we believe his lies, our conscience may *excuse* us rather than *accuse* us.

The subtlety, or snare, of deception is that we don't know when we are deceived, and that is always dangerous.

Many times secret, or pet, sins are hidden for years in a person's life—hidden from others, but not from God. A person may be in denial about them because God has allowed them to continue and they have not been struck with a lightning bolt. In their deceived state, they may think that God doesn't know about it or doesn't mind as long as the rest of their life is in order. They may be going to church regularly, living an upright life as far as the world is concerned. They may be doing all kinds of things that are pleasing to God, maybe even serving as a Sunday school teacher, deacon or even pastor a church.

If you are seeking freedom, but you are not willing to let go and deal with that pet sin, you rob both yourself and God. You are robbing yourself of the joy, faith and peace of mind that could be yours. You are robbing God of His ability to use you as completely as He wants to because strongholds in your life will keep you from being an effective witness to the rest of the world. Why would the rest of the world want to be like you if you constantly walk around with a frown on your face and a heavy spirit?

Sin alienates you from God. If you were willing to allow sin in your life, then you must be willing to give it up. You must draw the line. God can't do that for you.

Do not be deceived! Just because you have not been struck by lightning does not mean God approves of or condones your sin. It only proves that God is longsuffering, patient and loving with His children.

After He has given us time to change on our own, and we don't, He may go to extraordinary lengths to show us the error of our ways, to get us back on track!

Rebellion against God can manifest itself in many ways, but it always leads to a dead-end road. The bondage of rebellion, especially against God's specific word, can lead a person into all kinds of deception, false doctrines and heresies, which leads to a *stronghold of error*. This stronghold of error may come in very subtly. It not only existed in the early church, but it also exists in the church today, where many are held in the bondage of error. This can easily occur when a person is unstable, untaught or simply not grounded in the Word of God.

Proverbs 29:1 says, "He who is often rebuked, and hardens his neck, will suddenly be destroyed, and that without remedy." Rebellion and unsubmissiveness go hand in hand, and they can and do lead to a belief in false doctrines. False doctrines divide the church when people rebel against the truth of the Bible. There are many religions that are indeed keeping millions in slavery through false teaching they call "knowledge" that actually contradicts God's Word. But the Bible is the inspired Word of God, and we are to avoid anything that contradicts it. This includes any and all speculation that is not based on truth.

False teachers will lead you away from the truth if they themselves have been led away from the truth and are believing a lie. If a person is unteachable, argumentative, confused, or has a dullness of comprehension, he or she will be more susceptible to a stronghold of error in doctrine. In 1 Timothy 4:1 we see a warning about this very thing: "Now the Spirit expressly says that in latter times some will depart from the faith, giving heed to deceiving spirits and doctrines of demons." False doctrines will enslave and keep a person in bondage like nothing else can! God has not changed, nor has the Word of God changed! God and His Word are the same yesterday, today and forever!

God never wants us to continue in bondage (slavery) to the enemy. That enemy may very well be your flesh and lustful desires. We cannot blame our sins on the devil, because God gave us a free will to make the decisions and choices that either keep us free or in slavery. God will not be mocked, as we see in Galatians 6:7–8:

> Do not be deceived, God is not mocked; for whatever a man sows, that he will also reap. For

he who sows to his flesh will of the flesh reap corruption, but he who sows to the Spirit will of the Spirit reap everlasting life.

Know the truth—if you desire to be set free from slavery, the Holy Spirit will show you the areas that may be hindering your relationship with the Lord! Second Timothy 2:24–26 declares:

And a servant of the Lord must not quarrel but be gentle to all, able to teach, patient, in humility correcting those who are in opposition, if God perhaps will grant them repentance, so that they may know the truth, and that they may come to their senses and escape the snare of the devil, having been taken captive by him to do his will.

After doing a personal examination of yourself with the Holy Spirit's guidance, you may be able to identify areas of bondage in your own life from which you need to be set free. If you have identified a pet sin or a stronghold of error that is keeping you in bondage, and you truly want freedom, then you must do the following:

1. Be completely honest with yourself and with God.
2. Truly desire to be set free.
3. Know you are changed by the power of God's love.
4. Humbly submit to God.
5. Confess all known sins (including stubbornness and rebellion).
6. Renounce any involvement in any area that may be a stronghold of bondage or error.
7. Know you have a free will, and with God's help, you can begin to make the right choices.

Chapter Six

Dabbling/Curiosity

T IS POSSIBLE FOR PEOPLE TO HAVE A CURSE IN operation in their lives and not know it. They know that something is controlling them, but they don't know how to deal with it. They may try to deal with it by getting counseling or taking antidepressants, or going into denial. They may have prayed about it or had other people pray for them, but it keeps coming back. It may be something that has plagued them for as long as they can remember. This stronghold may be lying, stealing, rebellion against authority, laziness, stubbornness, gluttony or sexual perversion (to name a few). It may very well be something that was passed down from a previous generation.

Then, there are those who, *through their own actions,* have allowed strongholds to enter and take root from a seed they themselves planted—curiosity and dabbling. They unwittingly opened themselves up, and the foothold was granted, or implanted.

Next, the seed germinated and took root in its host. It was unchecked and allowed to mature, and the end result is a life that is out of control. The dabbling that was thought to be innocent when a person was just experimenting in drugs, alcohol, gambling or pornography resulted in addiction. The addiction is the curse and can lead to a host of other problems.

My experience over the years is that you can't always judge a book by its cover, nor can you see or know what may be controlling someone, or what may be prompting or motivating a person's behavior. While teaching some college courses at the University of Missouri and at Lindenwood College, I became acquainted with some very talented and intelligent students. Several that I personally knew took their own lives. *Why,* I asked? They each had bright futures ahead of them. For the sake of privacy, I will use first names only:

> *Tom:* He was an excellent artist, and creating artistic works came to him as easily as walking around the block. He was as talented an athlete as he was an artist. He won several state diving championships and had the potential to be a national competitor. He committed suicide. Later, I found out from some of his acquaintances that, indeed, he dabbled in drugs, which led to depression and later caused him to take his own life!

> *Charlie:* Talented in real estate and woodworking, he was married and had two very young children. He, too, dabbled in drugs, which led to fear and depression, and ulti-

mately, suicide.

Jim: Extremely talented as a musician, he fin-
ished college at a very young age and became
a high school music and band teacher. He was
an alcoholic and his alcoholism eventually
killed him.

All three were in their early prime of life, and all
three had secret strongholds that were allowed to
develop unchecked. The above examples are not
unique, and I could share many similar accounts of
individuals and families who "suffer through." If a
person allows a stronghold to go unchecked in his or
her life, that person will continue to suffer failure
and defeat. That person's life will be more difficult
than it has to be! I'm not saying your Christian walk
is always going to be easy, but I do believe many
people suffer needlessly. It's not just the person who
has the alcohol or drug problem that is affected—his
spouse and children suffer needlessly as well!

In our society today, it's called *dysfunctional* or
labeled as *codependency,* and it is a growing problem.
Back in the 1970s, the word *codependency* was coined
to refer to the families of those who had an alcohol
problem. Later, the term was expanded to refer to the
families of drug addicts as well. Today, the term has a
much broader use and refers to anyone in a significant
relationship with a person who has any kind of depen-
dency or obsession with alcohol, drugs, sex, food, work,
gambling, perfectionism, success, hobbies and so on. It
can be anything that causes that person to be abusive,
absent or physically or mentally impaired, thereby
depriving the loved ones of needed love and attention.

A codependent has been defined as one who has let another person's behavior affect him or her, and who is obsessed with controlling that person's behavior.

Now the experts are finding that codependent behavior is also showing up in children who come from divorced homes or other dysfunctional homes where there are addictions, eating disorders, sexual disorders, single parent, or a variety of verbal, physical or emotional abuses. Codependency is manifested in many different ways—none of them Christlike. Many books have been written on this subject. Even though many codependents are Christians, deception, abuse, neglect, and manipulation have scarred their lives. These scars, these characteristics, these strongholds are passed down to succeeding generations unless they are recognized and broken.

Every segment of our society is affected, from the rich to the poor, the low class to the high class, from the pulpit to the congregation, the religious to the non-religious. No one is exempt, not even our children!

Jesus said in John 8:32 "And you shall know the truth, and the truth shall make you free." Ask God right now—wherever you are—to reveal to you any area of your life that is subject to a stronghold. (Write it down.) We will put the spiritual ax to the root in later chapters. There is nothing you can name that is too difficult for God to break.

You may be reading this book and right now know in your heart that you have never accepted Jesus as Lord and Savior, or maybe you have only done so half-heartedly. If you have truly accepted Him in your heart, you will allow Him to heal all your hurts and lead you in making the right choices from this day forward. John 3:16 says, "For God so loved the world that He gave His only begotten Son, that whoever believes in Him should not perish but have everlasting life."

God is bigger than any mistake you have made—He is bigger than any mistake you can make. He can turn any mistake in your life into a miracle, if you let Him. If you believe that, then by faith, ask Him to come into your life right now! Pray this prayer (or a similar prayer in your own words) aloud:

> Dear God,
> I really don't know You, but I would like to be set free from sin. I admit I am a sinner, and I would like for you to forgive me and make me clean so that I can live a victorious life. I believe and I accept Jesus as my Savior. Jesus, come into my life and make me a child of God. Holy Spirit, give me the strength to be an overcomer. Thank You. Amen.

Chapter Seven

Generational Curses

E CANNOT CHOOSE OUR PARENTS ANY MORE THAN we can choose our sex, race or skin color. However, just as we carry genes of our parents that give us their physical traits—height, color of skin, hair or eyes—we may also carry any spiritual baggage they may have had in their lives, such as (but not limited to) the following:

- Involvement in witchcraft or the occult
- Abuse of drugs or alcohol
- Uncontrolled anger or violence
- Rebellious, stubborn attitude
- Physical, verbal or emotional abuse
- Sexual sin or perversion
- Laziness, gluttony, confusion, fear or tendency to worry
- Sickness or disease—heart problems, diabetes, cancer, arthritis, etc.
- The effect of profanity or negative words spoken directly to a person or about a person

The words or actions of a person in authority carry a lot of clout (power). This will be discussed in greater detail in chapter 10. The power of a parent can have a profound effect on his or her children, in either a positive or negative way. The power in and of the words we speak can change lives forever, even affecting future generations as we see in Genesis 9:20–27. Noah's sin is described as follows:

> And Noah began to be a farmer, and he planted a vineyard. Then he drank of the wine and was drunk, and became uncovered in his tent. And Ham, the father of Canaan, saw the nakedness of his father, and told his two brothers outside. But Shem and Japheth took a garment, laid it on both their shoulders, and went backward and covered the nakedness of their father. Their faces were turned away, and they did not see their father's nakedness.
>
> So Noah awoke from his wine, and knew what his younger son had done to him. Then he said: "Cursed be Canaan; a servant of servants he shall be to his brethren."
>
> And he said: "Blessed be the Lord, the God of Shem, and may Canaan be his servant. May God enlarge Japheth, and may he dwell in the tents of Shem; and may Canaan be his servant."

The Scripture described this scene for us: Noah awoke from a drunken stupor, half hung over, and somehow he either knew or he found out from his younger two sons, Shem and Japheth, what Ham had done. Ham may have just been in the wrong place at the wrong time. It's not clear and there are no defined details as to exactly what happened at the house of Noah!

What is clear is that Noah sinned when he spoke against the family of Ham, his eldest son. He cursed what God had blessed—his own family! Whether it was frustration or anger or the effect of the alcohol, it is not clear. Noah did not take his frustration out on the guilty one, Ham, but for some reason directed his wrath instead to his innocent grandson, Canaan, the son of Ham. Canaan had nothing to do with the entire matter, yet Noah prophesied (spoke) against Canaan, and a powerful curse was shackled around the necks of untold future generations, nations of people who are still suffering and/or subject to *bondage.* This happened all because one man sinned by cursing! Neither Canaan nor the future generations deserved to be cursed, yet they were! In like manner, a father or mother today can curse future generations, or someone may have cursed them long ago, and it is now manifesting itself in their children.

Again, in the first of the Ten Commandments, we see how the sins of previous generations can affect future generations:

> "You shall have no other gods before Me. You shall not make for yourself a carved image—any likeness of anything that is in heaven above, or is in the earth beneath, or that is in the water under the earth; you shall not bow down to them nor serve them. For I, the Lord your God, am a jealous God, *visiting the iniquity of the fathers upon the children to the third and fourth generations of those who hate Me."*
>
> —EXODUS 20:3–5, EMPHASIS ADDED

Exodus 20:5 and Exodus 34:7 both indicate that evil—wickedness, rebellion and hate—manifested in people who obviously despised God's will and would not repent would cause the generational curse(s) to be passed on.

The commandment, "You shall have no other gods before Me" was given to Moses on Mount Sinai to give to the children of Israel. They had just been delivered from Egypt, where the inhabitants worshiped numerous gods, such as sun god, moon god and so on. They had gods for everything, and they worshiped and gave honor to all of them. Many nations of the world today still have large numbers of gods they worship, rather than the one and only God Almighty.

Christian nations for the most part do not worship pagan gods but, in effect, have gods of silver and gold—material wealth, houses, automobiles, yachts, etc. Anything a person idolizes and allows to have a higher priority than God can be considered idolatry. For example, if material wealth keeps us from being dependent on God, then it becomes a problem. God is opposed to our being greedy for, obsessive about or controlled by material things. If your family wealth was obtained through greed or by illegal means, there is probably a curse attached to it.

Please understand, I do not believe God is opposed to our having material wealth, for it is God who enables us to obtain those things, as we see in the following scriptures:

> "Then you say in your heart, 'My power and the might of my hand have gained me this wealth.' And you shall remember the Lord your God, for it is He who gives you power to get wealth . . . "
> —Deuteronomy 8:17–18

35

> As for every man to whom God has given riches
> and wealth, and given him power to eat of it, to
> receive his heritage and rejoice in his labor—
> this is the gift of God.
>
> —ECCLESIASTES 5:19

As you can see, we can and do pass on physical traits and habits, curses and blessings, sickness and health, poverty and wealth. Familiar spirits (which we will discuss in the next chapter), often are the evil force behind the spiritual heredity that can cause a generational curse. Many people will argue that your heredity is either biological (genes from your father and mother) or environmental influence (what you heard and saw the people in your family saying or doing). Although secular physicians and psychologists usually recognize biological and environmental heredity, what they usually do not recognize is the role of the spirit in heredity.

The Bible reveals that man is body, soul and spirit. Even as biological and environmental heredity affect the body, so spiritual heredity affects your soul and spirit. Body, soul and spirit are intertwined. It is impossible to separate them while we are living in the flesh.

If the real problem is spiritual, and scientists, physicians, psychologists, and even theologians refuse to recognize it as such, they will probably never solve the problem. The best they can hope to do is treat the symptoms.

There are spiritual forces behind inherited criminal behavior, hereditary illness and recurring social problems. As we have said repeatedly, the Bible describes such forces as curses or strongholds of Satan.

Oftentimes society looks at drug addicts, rapists and the sexually perverse as degenerates. We must stop looking at the flesh and look at the person's spiritual background. The spiritual forces behind that person may have been so strong, they simply were unable to make the right choice. They may have been driven by a force they could neither identify nor control.

God is faithful, merciful and full of love, and He wants to deliver that person and set him free. John 3:17 declares, "For God did not send the Son into the world in order to judge (to reject, to condemn, to pass sentence on) the world, but that the world might find salvation and be made safe and sound through Him" (AMP). The only way to be free from any generational curse (if God does not sovereignly deliver you) is to *renounce* the curse and apply the bondage-breaking power of the *blood* of Jesus. There is no other solution—there is no greater power!

Chapter Eight

Familiar Spirits

AMILIAR SPIRIT MAY BE AN OLD TESTAMENT TERM, but all of us have seen familiar spirits in operation in today's society. A familiar spirit can be a spirit of divination or its medium.

The King James translation uses the words *familiar spirit* sixteen times. The literal translation of the Hebrew words is "knowing spirit." Following are the key facts to know about familiar spirits.

1. A familiar spirit is an evil spirit that becomes familiar with an individual or family. It follows that person or family and knows their weaknesses—physically, mentally, spiritually and emotionally.

2. A familiar spirit cannot read your mind or know your thoughts, but it does know about you.

3. A spirit that is familiar with you will communicate knowledge about you to those whom

they serve. Not every person who has supernatural knowledge about you is of God, as we
see in Acts 16:16–19:

> Now it happened, as we went to prayer, that a
> certain slave girl possessed with a spirit of div-
> ination met us, who brought her masters much
> profit by fortune-telling. This girl followed Paul
> and us, and cried out, saying, "These men are
> the servants of the Most High God, who pro-
> claim to us the way of salvation." And this she
> did for many days. But Paul, greatly annoyed,
> turned and said to the spirit, "I command you in
> the name of Jesus Christ to come out of her."
> And he came out that very hour.

If someone, such as a psychic, tells you things about
your life that they had no natural way of knowing,
there's a good chance a familiar spirit is in operation.

A familiar spirit is familiar with an individual or
family's sins. It knows what buttons to push on each
family member. It knows every weakness and almost
every thing about each family member, in order to
influence each of them to sin. Through sin, the curse
is passed on. A familiar spirit can be with a family for
generations. It is passed on to future generations who
also sin, which allows the same spirit to transcend
several generations.

For example, if your father or mother was an alcoholic or drug abuser, those evil spirits will watch you.
They know that you probably already inherited a
weakness for alcohol or drugs, and they will drive you
crazy. If you have children, they will be ready to
attack them, too. They try to get each generation
involved in the same sin, so they can carry the curse

on and on. These spirits that control the parents frequently control the children, and, many times, the manifestations of the stronghold are much worse in the succeeding generations. Their control can grow with each passing generation.

The Old Testament warns about familiar spirits. Leviticus 19:31 says, "Give no regard to mediums and familiar spirits; do not seek after them, to be defiled by them: I am the Lord your God." Leviticus 20:6 reads, "And the person who turns to mediums and familiar spirits, to prostitute himself with them, I will set My face against that person and cut him off from his people."

Many people consult mediums, clairvoyants and spirits to gain knowledge about the future. They think they are receiving information from the spirit of a loved one or from the spirit of a person who has passed from this life to death. One cannot call up a spirit of a deceased person. (No one can except Jesus Christ himself.) That spirit that has been conjured up by someone in the occult practice of necromancy is an evil, lying spirit. It may know things about the past, but it can't predict the future. It may know things about you or your circumstances, but that is what a familiar spirit is all about. It will give you enough truth to hook you into thinking it is good, and then fill you with lies to destroy you. There is no such thing as a "good" familiar spirit.

A familiar spirit may enter a person through his or her involvement in occult practices, condemning that person by his or her own actions.

Many of the ills of our society are caused by involvement in occult practices, such as witchcraft, fortunetellers and psychics. These practices open the door to a life that is subject to numerous strongholds/curses. *Disobedience opens the door.*

YOU CAN PULL DOWN THE STRONGHOLD

WHEN JESUS DIED ON CALVARY, HE NOT ONLY DIED FOR our sins; He also redeemed us from the curse of the law. Jesus became the curse so we might be blessed. *We do not have to live under or accept the curse imposed by our own sin, the sins of our ancestors, or evil words spoken over us.* We can and must use the power of the blood, which was the shedding of Jesus' blood at Calvary, and reverse any and all curses upon us. As we saw in the account of Passover in Exodus 12:1–7, the blood of the lamb did nothing until that blood was applied to the door of the house. When the destroyer saw the blood, he would not come near.

We are the *house*—the temple of the Holy Spirit. If the enemy has entered your house, is setting up shop, and seemingly has free reign in your life, you must identify the source of the *open door.* Remember that a stronghold is any area in your life where the enemy has established a dwelling place. As a born-again Christian, you must identify the opening.

- Was it sin?
- Was it disobedience?
- Was it dabbling?
- Was it a curse from an outside source?

SPIRITUAL WARFARE REQUIRES SPIRITUAL WEAPONS!

1. *You have to take charge—use your authority.*
   Webster's dictionary defines authority as 1) "the power or right to give commands, to take action and 2) power of influence, resulting from knowledge." Jesus says in Luke 10:19, "Behold, I give you the authority to trample on serpents and scorpions, and over all the power of the enemy, and nothing shall by any means hurt you."

2. *You must truly repent of all sin and disobedience and ask for forgiveness. Then you must believe you receive forgiveness and accept it.*
   First John 1:9 states, "If we confess our sins, He is faithful and just to forgive us our sins and to cleanse us from all unrighteousness."

3. *You must renounce any strongholds or curses.*
   Second Corinthians 4:2 says, "But we have renounced the hidden things of shame . . . "

4. *You must bind the enemy and cast him out.*
   According to Matthew 18:18, "Whatever you bind on earth will be bound in heaven, and whatever you loose on earth will be loosed in heaven."

5. *Visualize and announce that you are applying the blood of Jesus over yourself and family.*
   "For all have sinned and fall short of the glory of God, being justified freely by His grace through the redemption that is in Christ Jesus, whom God set forth as a propitiation *by His blood, through faith,* to demonstrate His righteousness" (Rom. 3:23–25, emphasis added).

In chapter 20, "Identify the Strongholds," many strongholds are listed, along with their manifestations. At the end of that chapter are sample prayers for breaking generational curses or any type of addiction, and tearing down strongholds. If at any time in your life the Holy Spirit reveals there is something hindering your Christian walk, you can use the following sample prayer to break any and all strongholds that have developed because of your own sin or disobedience. (Always pray out loud.)

Heavenly Father,

I ask for forgiveness for _____, _____, _____ (name any and all sins or disobedience) in my life.

I repent of _____, _____, _____ (those sins or disobedience). I take charge and use my authority as a born-again believer. I bind the enemy (Satan and all the forces of evil) and cast him out of my life, and I apply the blood of Jesus (visualize the covering and the power of the blood) over myself, my family, my home, automobiles, etc. In Jesus' name, I pray. Amen.

Chapter Nine

False Prophets and False Prophesying

WHAT IS A FALSE PROPHET? IT IS A RELIGIOUS imposter, a foreteller, who speaks erroneous doctrine and lies. This type of person is often very smooth and deceptive.

The Old Testament speaks of false prophets, and we are warned about them several times in the New Testament. Jesus warns us to be aware of false prophets in Matthew 7:15–23:

> Beware of false prophets, who come to you in sheep's clothing, but inwardly they are ravenous wolves. You will know them by their fruits. Do men gather grapes from thornbushes or figs from thistles? Even so, every good tree bears good fruit, but a bad tree bears bad fruit. A good tree cannot bear bad fruit, nor can a bad tree bear good fruit. Every tree that does not bear good fruit is cut down and thrown into the fire. Therefore by their fruits you will know them.
>
> Not everyone who says to Me, "Lord, Lord,"

shall enter the kingdom of heaven, but he who does the will of My Father in heaven. Many will say to Me in that day, "Lord, Lord, have we not prophesied in Your name, cast out demons in Your name, and done many wonders in Your name?' And then I will declare to them, "I never knew you; depart from Me, you who practice lawlessness!"

Jesus clearly emphasized several points here:

1. In verse 15, Jesus referred to prophets who knew the Lord at one time before wickedness corrupted them. These are the ones who are (spiritually) very dangerous, using their position of authority, flagrantly defying the will of God.

2. Even though these false prophets were prophesying, casting out demons and doing many wonders in Jesus' name, they may have had character flaws or some strongholds in their lives that were never dealt with, and consequently, they fell into error.

3. Jesus described them as wolves in sheep's clothing. You can be sure that when Jesus attaches a name like wolf or viper to a person, it's pretty serious, and should get our full attention. He is saying they may look like sheep and act like sheep, but they aren't sheep. He says they are ravenous "inwardly," which means they are out to extort or plunder. Instead of giving to the flock, their intent is to get from the flock.

4. Remember, you will know them by their fruits (results)—or their lack of them—good or bad.

5. Jesus said that a bad tree does not produce good fruit. So by their results, you will know them. Does their life line up with God's Word? Do they have the fruit of the spirit (Gal. 5:22–23) in their life?

Again in Matthew 24:11, Jesus said, "Then many false prophets will rise up and deceive many." False prophets were present before and during the time when Jesus physically lived and walked on this earth. But here in Matthew 24:11, Jesus is specifically speaking to His disciples about what to look for before the end of the age and just prior to His Second Coming.

False prophets come in many shapes and forms—to corrupt, plunder and deceive. Their purpose is to deceive, and they are doing it very well! These so-called prophets of God are twisting the truth. They feed on the fears and ignorance of those who are not grounded in the Word.

The main difference between the false prophets of old and those of today is that today's prophets are more sophisticated and have radio and television at their disposal. Consequently, they are able to reach many more people. Most pastors will not allow these so-called prophets to operate in their churches, so hotel and banquet centers are often rented instead. In this way, they are able to draw people from more than one local church. (Please do not misunderstand—I am not saying that anyone who rents a hotel or banquet center for a spiritual or religious meeting is a false prophet. Sometimes it's simply a matter of convenience or some other legitimate reason.)

Oftentimes, people are drawn to these activities,

hoping to get a personal prophecy about their own lives, whether it's true or not! The false prophet will give misinformation, for example, predicting that true believers in Jesus Christ have reason to panic rather than having a perfect peace about events in the future, particularly concerning the Great Tribulation. This doom and gloom will cause fear and doubt to enter a person's heart, robbing them of their peace and trust in God to protect them.

The panic that was spread about the Y2K computer scare caused many to fear for the worst, including Christians, who stockpiled food, water, generators, etc. I'm not saying it was wrong to take some precautions, but what I am saying is if you are trusting in the arm of the flesh instead of having faith in the Lord, it's contrary to the Word of God—no matter what the circumstances.

God gave us about seven thousand promises in His Word, and you can always count on God to keep His promises to us. When a person receives Jesus as their Lord and is born again, this means that person is saved. But salvation encompasses more than a ticket to heaven—a whole lot more! It includes deliverance, safety, preservation, healing, soundness and more. It is God's grace that saved us, and it is God's grace that will keep us. It is when one comes out from under the umbrella of grace or out of God's will that one gets into trouble.

It is not God's will for us to be running all over the country just to get a word from the Lord when we can do that ourselves right where we are. The Holy Spirit will communicate to us through the written Word of God (the Bible), sometimes by the spoken word through a preacher or Christian friend, sometimes by the still small voice we hear inside, and sometimes through the prophetic word. If it is through the prophetic word, it is usually confirmed by more than one source. This confirmation can possibly come through another person (someone who operates in word of wisdom or word of knowledge) or it may be confirmation in your heart of something the Lord has already been speaking to you.

We can fall into error when we listen to the wrong voice, hear and accept the wrong preaching or follow the wrong teaching. By doing so, we allow ourselves to be an open target for the enemy.

A person who operates in the gift of prophecy can start out right, sincere and with good intentions. But if somehow they allow a foothold in their life and don't "nip it in the bud," they can begin to operate in a spirit of error. This can happen to anyone, especially someone who is not fully aware of the snares, traps and subtleties of the devil. So be on guard and beware! This spirit of error or deception has happened to many and is often caused by their own selfish attitudes of lust, greed, jealousy or pride. Sometimes it is because of just plain ignorance or stubbornness, a refusal to hear or accept the truth. I have seen this sort of thing split churches and send people off in the wrong direction in their lives, leading many astray. Although God's words are true, the gifts operate through human vessels—imperfect men and women who may be subject to error.

So—test the spirits! If the word or prophecy does not line up with the Word of God, throw it out! Your "discerner" will know. A true prophet or prophetess of God (a true Holy Spirit-gifted believer) will not lead you against God's will but, in fact, will exhort, edify and comfort you and/or the church. The gifts will be operated in love and will always line up with God's Word! There are many solid ministries out there that do just that.

Just because a person operates in the gift of prophecy does not necessarily mean they are called to the office or ministry of prophet, but a prophet who is called to that office will always operate in the gift of prophecy.

Jesus Himself established the office of the prophet when He established the five-fold ministry, and at no time since then has He done away with that ministry position. However, there are those who would argue that true prophets don't exist in our day and time. The truth is, the prophet under the New Testament does exist, but this office does not have the same status as the prophet under the Old Testament.

Under the old covenant (Old Testament), people went to the prophet for guidance because only the king, the priest and the prophet were anointed by the Spirit of God to stand in their respective offices. The rest of the people had no tangible presence of God in their lives. The presence of God was shut up in the Holy of Holies. They didn't have the Spirit of God either on them or in them, so the people would go to the prophet for guidance.

Under the New Covenant, it is unscriptural for one to seek guidance through the ministry of the prophet. The ministry of the prophet today serves a different function. Anyone who stands in this office today

49

should be there because he has a divine calling on his life—the same as the other four offices.

Jesus established the office of the prophet, as well as the other offices—apostle, evangelist, pastor and teacher—as we see in Ephesians 4:10–15 below:

> He who descended is also the One who ascended far above all the heavens, that He might fill all things.) And He Himself gave some to be apostles, some prophets, some evangelists, and some pastors and teachers, for the equipping of the saints for the work of the ministry, for the edifying of the body of Christ, till we all come to the unity of the faith and of the knowledge of the Son of God, to a perfect man, to the measure of the stature of the fullness of Christ; that we should no longer be children, tossed to and fro and carried about with every wind of doctrine, by the trickery of men, in the cunning craftiness of deceitful plotting, but, speaking the truth in love, may grow up in all things into Him who is the head—Christ . . .

The true prophet is a preacher or a teacher of the Word and is called to full-time ministry. He or she must have a consistent manifestation of at least two of the revelation gifts (word of wisdom, word of knowledge or discerning of spirits) plus the gift of prophecy. A prophet is one who has visions and can bring forth revelations. Sometimes he does operate as a foreteller through the gift of the word of wisdom.

Jesus Himself gave all five ministry offices to the body, the church (v. 11). Why? Verse 12 says the purpose was to equip the saints—past, present and future—to edify (or build up) the church. They are the architects or the builders of the church as directed by the Lord, via the anointing of the Holy Spirit. These are very gifted men and women of God. Verse 13 says this work continues "till we *all* come to the unity of the faith." Have all born-again believers come to the unity of the faith, in other words, oneness? You don't have to look very far to realize we are not there yet. Have we all become perfected and mature in Christ yet? Not yet, but I believe we are going to get there soon because I believe He is coming soon.

When we get to the point where we are not moved by every wind of doctrine, and when we recognize the trickery and deceitfulness of men, and when we speak the truth in love and grow up and know who we are in Christ, then we will see the greatest outpouring the world will ever witness on planet Earth other than the Second Coming of Jesus!

It will take the recognition and acceptance of the five-fold ministry working together to fulfill the Great Commission. There is no distinction given by God's Word that indicates in any way that any of the ministry offices have been done away with. Either the list stands complete as Christ set it up or it doesn't stand at all. Nowhere along the line did He come along and delete part of it! Only man could have done that. When the church is fully mature, then we can say the job of the five-fold ministry is complete.

CONCERNING SPIRITUAL GIFTS

IN MARK 16:15–18, JESUS GAVE A COMMAND, AND WITH that command He gave authority and equipped by His Spirit those who believe and follow His directions:

> Go into all the world and preach the gospel to

every creature. He who believes and is baptized will be saved; but he who does not believe will be condemned. And these signs will follow those who believe: In My name they will cast out demons; they will speak with new tongues; they will take up serpents; and if they drink anything deadly, it will by no means hurt them; they will lay hands on the sick and they will recover.

In order to operate effectively in the directive Jesus gave here in Mark 16, we would, out of necessity, need to be equipped in order to produce the results Jesus said we would have!

This requires supernatural power operating in believers! We are the vessels God works through. First Corinthians 12:8–10 describes the gifts that are given to those who are filled with the Holy Spirit. This "filling" is the baptism in the Holy Spirit and is a separate experience from water baptism. (See Matthew 3:11 where John the Baptist talked about how he baptized with water but that one mightier than he—Jesus—would be coming after him and would baptize believers with the Holy Spirit and with fire.) This experience can take place at the same time as water baptism, it can happen at the moment one decides to receive salvation, or it can happen at any time after the salvation experience.

However, if you have never received the baptism in the Holy Spirit, you will not receive any of the spiritual gifts spoken of in 1 Corinthians 12:8–10, or the supernatural power that comes with these gifts. The Holy Spirit imparts spiritual gifts to each of us individually as "He wills" (v. 11). These gifts are primarily given for the benefit (edification) of the entire church, not for an individual's own use. They are freely given and are not to be used for personal gain. And, furthermore, they must all be operated in love, or they profit us nothing (as it says in 1 Cor. 13).

I believe that if a person is trying to operate in the gifts of the Spirit but doesn't have the fruit of the Spirit, it's quite likely he or she may operate in error in the gifts. Just to clarify:

The fruit of the Spirit is found in Galatians 5:22–23 as follows:

> "But the fruit of the Spirit is love, joy, peace, longsuffering, kindness, goodness, faithfulness, gentleness, self-control. Against such there is no law."

The gifts of the Spirit are found in 1 Corinthians 12:8–10 as follows:

> "for to one is given the word of wisdom through the Spirit, to another the word of knowledge through the same Spirit, to another faith by the same Spirit, to another gifts of healings by the same Spirit, to another prophecy, to another discerning of spirits, to another different kinds of tongues, to another the interpretation of tongues."

Ministries should be based on and built around the entire Word of God, rather than primarily focused on the spiritual gifts. The ministry of the gospel should always take priority. The gifts will follow!

God has promised to give each of us wisdom. James

53

1:5 says, "If any of you lacks wisdom, let him ask of God, who gives to all liberally and without reproach, and it will be given to him." We are never to quit our job, divorce our spouse, give away our home, turn over our money or marry someone just because a person tells us "they are hearing from God."

People who are endeavoring to control other people's lives through personal prophecy have ulterior motives, and God does not honor that. God can and does speak to each of us through His Spirit—the Holy Spirit. If you don't have a peace about something someone has told you, use good, sound judgment, pray before you act, and seek Godly counselors.

A true prophet of God and those operating according to the spiritual gifts will not only edify, exhort and comfort, but they may also give a word (direction and correction) that some may not like to hear. It should be done in love in order to keep them on track and in the will of God. It may be the very word that will set one's life in order and on the right track. *It will often be confirmation of what the Holy Spirit is already telling that person!* God does not sugarcoat His word, nor should those who are gifted to deliver it, even when it's a difficult thing to administer to the person or persons who are receiving it.

Chapter Ten

The Power of Your Words

OUR WORDS ARE POWERFUL—I'M NOT SURE ANY of us realize just how powerful! Your words can carry the creative power of God or the destructive power of the devil. They can encourage or discourage, heal or hurt, build up or tear down. Depending on whether you speak a blessing or a curse over your family, the words you speak will produce either good or harmful results. When a curse is spoken over someone, it can result in a spiritual stronghold in that person's life or on his or her family. Strongholds or curses, as discussed in previous chapters, can be passed on to future generations. Blessings can be passed on the same way.

Most people readily accept the concept of blessings as valid or biblical, but they are either skeptical about, or refuse to believe, that curses can be passed on as easily. In most cultures, a curse is viewed as something a witch, warlock, or practitioner of voodoo would conjure up and place on someone. In truth, they can. But the Bible says that we all have the power in our tongues to both bless and curse! Deuteronomy 30:19 declares, "I have set before you life and death, blessing and cursing; therefore choose life, that both you and your descendants may live."

A curse means to *speak* evil over, pray against or wish evil against a person or thing. To curse someone with negative, condemning words can cause hardships and failure in that person's life. The word *curse* occurs over two hundred times in the Bible. In the beginning, God blessed all His creation, including man. It wasn't until the fall of Adam that we read the first recorded account of a curse in Genesis 3:14–17. (See chapter 1.)

*Words give place to the enemy of our soul,
and he will use them!*

Ephesians 4:27 warns, "nor give place to the devil." The Bible gives explicit warnings about giving place, or residence, to Satan to operate in your life or the lives of others. Don't give your enemy a foothold! When you give place to Satan, you open up your spirit, and Satan will take advantage of the open door. If you give him an inch, he will take a mile. Captivity results! You can easily become a slave, held by the shackles of that sin and disobedience.

The forces that determine all events in this world fall into two categories: visible and invisible. Blessings and curses are invisible forces, or spiritual powers, which are transmitted by our *words*. Ask yourself, "Do I want what I just said to come to pass?" Words spoken to someone or about someone can become an invisible force that is passed on to future generations. Prejudice and hate are passed down from generation to generation by the words that come out of our mouths.

BE ACCOUNTABLE FOR YOUR WORDS

JESUS SAID IN MATTHEW 12:36–37, "BUT I TELL YOU, ON the day of judgment men will have to give account for every idle (inoperative, nonworking) word they speak. For by your words you will be justified and acquitted, and by your words you will be condemned and sentenced" (AMP). Why did He say we would be judged by our words? There is power in the tongue! In Proverbs 18:21 we read, "Death and life are in the power of the tongue, and those who love it will eat its fruit." Do not be rash (reckless) with your words and let not your heart utter anything hastily before God!

"Sticks and stones may break my bones, but words will never harm me." This little rhyme was used when I was a child (and is still used today) as a defense against the pain of cutting words spoken to us by another person. But saying that words cannot hurt or harm us does not change reality. To deny that words can harm is to deny the truth. The Bible teaches us that words are powerful spiritual forces that affect every area of our lives. Ask any marriage counselor if words can destroy marriages. Marriages dissolve every day because of hurtful words (usually spoken over a period of time) that wound the other person. The marriage can also be adversely affected due to the scars of word wounds that one or both spouses received from their parents while they were children.

Never expect your marriage partner to heal the wounds from your childhood—only God can do that!

Time heals wounds, but the scars remain with that person for a lifetime. Many times the same cutting, stabbing words are used over and over again. It's like opening the old scar and pouring salt in the wound—it hurts! Sometimes the scars are small and healed over, and other times they are large, open wounds that never completely heal. The person on the receiving end of those hurtful words may either develop low self-esteem or become bitter and hostile, taking out their hostility on innocent people around them. Word scars produce anger, resentment, hate and bitterness that can eventually destroy relationships.

Parents and authority figures, including teachers, law enforcement officials and government officials, all have some measure of authority over all of us. Those in authority should be particularly careful to choose their words. If a parent or other person in authority tells a child he or she is stupid and that child *accepts* and *believes* those words are true, a very negative effect has been imposed on that child. In the same way, people in any relationship can and do condemn each other.

When you tell someone he is stupid and will never amount to anything, (or any words of that nature,) you are actually pronouncing a condemnation or curse over them. You are setting in motion a destructive force that can continue from generation to generation unless it is supernaturally broken.

I have heard teachers talk about students in ways that would make a parent cringe. "That student is a good-for-nothing troublemaker. He is rotten to the core and will never amount to anything worthwhile." They have put negative words into motion that may condemn that child to failure. And then, later on, when the problem is intensified, the teacher wonders, *What got into that child?*

Negative, critical, judgmental words of condemnation are all around us, particularly in the political, governmental arenas. Is it any wonder that our nation seems more divided politically than ever before, with more slander, backbiting and hostility than ever?

TONGUE OF FIRE

IN JAMES 3:1–11, WE SEE THAT THE TONGUE IS CALLED AN unruly evil:

> My brethren, let not many of you become teachers, knowing that we shall receive a stricter judgment. For we all stumble in many things. If anyone does not stumble in word, he is a perfect man, able also to bridle the whole body. Indeed, we put bits in horses' mouths that they may obey us, and we turn their whole body. Look also at ships: although they are so large and are driven by fierce winds, they are turned by a very small rudder wherever the pilot desires. Even so the tongue is a little member and boasts great things.
>
> See how great a forest a little fire kindles! And the tongue is a fire, a world of iniquity. The tongue is so set among our members that it defiles the whole body, and sets on fire the course of nature; and it is set on fire by hell. For every kind of beast and bird, of reptile and creature of the sea, is tamed and has been tamed by mankind. But no man can tame the tongue. It is an unruly evil, full of deadly poison. With it we bless our God and Father, and with it we curse

men, who have been made in the similitude of God. Out of the same mouth proceed blessing and cursing. My brethren, these things ought not to be so. Does a spring send forth fresh water and bitter from the same opening?

James wrote this epistle to the church that was dispersed all over the Roman Empire. Obviously, there was a serious problem that needed to be addressed. They were talking out of both sides of their mouths at the same time. This "tongue" thing needed to be corrected. James addressed the problem head on—he did not "tickle their ears" or try to make them feel good by soft-soaping the issue. In other words, James "rocked the boat." The church had settled into worldly things—they were talking and acting no differently than those around them.

Nothing has changed—the same can be said of the church today. If growth and maturity in our spiritual walk with God are desired, then one must take seriously these words that have been written to us. We have a disobedient tongue when we say things that are out of line with the Word of God. If you say something without thinking and then say, "Oh, I really didn't mean that," just remember that the world of the spirit realm doesn't operate on what you mean—it operates on what you say. So, say what you mean and mean what you say.

In verses 5 and 6 above, the tongue is referred to as a fire. A great forest fire is started from a single spark. When the fire is spent and you're left with all the ashes, it is almost impossible to find the spot where the spark ignited the blaze. The damage is done, and one may never know where it started. In the same way, the fire of a spoken word can cause great damage, leaving lives in ashes and ruin, and again, one may never know how or where it all started. The words put in motion today may not affect lives until years later.

In verses 6 and 8 we read, "And the tongue is a fire, a world of iniquity. The tongue is so set among our members that it defiles the whole body, and sets on fire the course of nature; and it is set on fire by hell," and, "No man can tame the tongue. It is an unruly evil, full of deadly poison." One would be hard-pressed to make a stronger statement pertaining to the tongue. The word *fire* used in the beginning of verse 6 is not like that of a match. It refers to a much stronger power, like that of lightning. It is obvious that lightning, once in motion, cannot be stopped or controlled. Lightning strikes from every direction, is indiscriminate, destructive and extremely powerful—even deadly! The tongue is compared to lightning—unpredictable, unrestrainable and destructive.

In verse 9 James goes on to say, "With it we bless our God and Father and with it we curse men, who have been made in the similitude [likeness] of God." In verse 10, "Out of the same mouth proceed blessing and cursing. My brethren, these things ought not to be so." This rebuke is given to all of us. These verses are clear—we have the power in our tongue to bless or curse.

WORDS OF FAITH

JAMES LEAVES NO QUESTION AS TO THE POWER WE HOLD WITHIN our tongues, but that power can either work for us, or it can work against us. There is no storm on life's sea through which we cannot safely sail by proper use of the rudder that is in our mouths. Our tongues can be a powerful tool used in our favor, but they can also be an unruly and deadly force, causing our lives to be ship-wrecked if we let them run out of control.

When the pressure is on, we really find out what is on the inside of us—and is often not the Word of God. However, our only hope for taming the tongue is the Word of God. Jesus warned in Mark 4 that Satan comes to steal the Word of God from our hearts through persecution, offense, the cares of this world, the deceitfulness of riches, and lust of other things. He uses anything and everything in this nat-ural realm to stir up our flesh and get us to open our mouths in a negative way.

If Satan can get our tongues, then he can get the rest of us. All he has to do is get us to lie against the truth, which is God's Word.

Don't expect to live your life in a positive way, if you are always saying negative things about yourself, your health or your finances! Nobody with a nega-tive attitude and a negative mouth will ever see their hopes and dreams come to pass.

We set the course of our own future. Our health, our wealth, as well as where we will spend eternity is "in our mouths." Romans 10:10 says, "For with the heart one believes unto righteousness, and *with the mouth* confession is made unto salvation" (emphasis added).

Everything about us has been, and will be, deter-mined by the words we speak. We can say we have faith, but unless we speak faith-filled words, our faith is useless. Negative words will negate our faith. It's the words that come from the heart that produce results. The person who just throws in a couple of faith words now and then isn't speaking them from the "abundance of his heart" (Matt. 12:34), so they are not effective.

God spoke the world into being through His word, and through it the sun, the moon and the stars are kept in place. His spoken word brought all living things into being and continues to produce life. By His word God pulls down kings and raises up nations. Through His word He blesses and saves, judges and destroys.

We were created in the image and likeness of God. We have the power to call those things that be not as though they were. We have the power to pull down strongholds, the power to bind and loose, the power of life and death in our mouths!

Pre-Identification

By now you may have already identified a curse or stronghold in operation in your own life.

- It may have come through a generational curse, through a familiar spirit, from negative words spoken about or to you, or from your own sin or disobedience.
- You may have accepted and believed the negative words spoken about or to you by a teacher or parent—words that said you will never amount to anything and you are no good, that you are ugly, stupid or undesirable. Your parents may have even declared, "I wish you were never born." Fear of rejection may be a stronghold in your life as a result of those words.
- You may have realized that you are perpetuating the curse by the words you are speaking

over someone, especially a child. You may have placed on your children the same curse you received—that they are no good, stupid, ugly and will never amount to anything.

- It may be a certain physical affliction or poverty that you have been told "runs" in your family. You may have been told that you have inherited a tendency toward the afflictions of cancer, heart trouble, alcoholism and so on. (If so, you may be condemning yourself by saying, "I'll probably get cancer, or I'll probably be poor the rest of my life.")

Once again, the spiritual realm doesn't operate on what you mean—it operates on what you say.

No matter what particular situation or circumstance we find ourselves in, we must become spiritually violent enough to rescue ourselves, our families and all that pertains to us from Satan's evil clutches. There is power in the blood and in the name of Jesus. Both of these are spiritual forces. You have the authority as a born-again believer to use these spiritual forces to take by force that which was stolen away from you.

God wants "priests and kings" on His throne. He desires health, protection, safety and blessing for His children—perfection in the body of his creation. Woe to rebellious children who execute their own plans, for in their ignorance they attempt to find solutions without turning to God. The battle is the Lord's, and it is to Him that we should turn as we identify strongholds in our own individual lives or in the lives of our family members.

64

Chapter Eleven

Blessings

E HAVE SEEN THAT BLESSINGS AND CURSES CAN come from the same mouth. Let's take a closer look at the power of blessings. The word *bless* occurs more than four hundred times in the Bible. It means to cause to be prosperous or to endow with health or prosperity, or to be happy. It literally means to be blessed in every area of one's life.

Just as a curse is transmitted by words, the Bible reveals that blessings can be passed on in the same way. The blessing is the release of the spoken word over another person or thing.

When God created the earth, sea creatures and birds, He spoke blessings over them, and they were blessed (Gen. 1:22). Then He spoke blessings over man and he was blessed (Gen. 1:28). Only man had the power to bring a curse upon himself through the sin of disobedience.

After the destruction of the earth by water in Genesis 9:1, God blessed Noah and his sons. When

God made a covenant with Abraham, He not only blessed Abraham, but all the families of the earth, as we see here in Genesis 12:2–3:

> "I will make you a great nation;
> I will bless you
> And make your name great;
> And you shall be a blessing.
> I will bless those who bless you,
> And I will curse him who curses you;
> And in you all the families of the
> earth shall be blessed."

God spoke a blessing over Abraham that extends down through the centuries. As a born-again believer:

- Your family is a part of "all the families of the earth."
- You are heir to the promises of Abraham.
- You are an heir to the promises extended to Abraham.
- You are heir to the Abrahamic covenant.
- You are destined to receive the same blessings God spoke over Abraham and his family!

We see Jesus using the same concept of blessing in His Sermon on the Mount:

> Blessed are the poor in spirit . . . blessed are those who mourn . . . blessed are the meek . . . blessed are those who hunger and thirst for righteousness . . . blessed are the merciful . . . blessed are the pure in heart . . . blessed are the peacemakers . . . blessed are those who are persecuted for righteousness' sake.
> —MATTHEW 5:3–10

66

Jesus taught that we should extend the blessings to others, even to our enemies, "Bless those who curse you, and pray for those who spitefully use you" (Luke 6:28). This may be one of the most difficult things for us to do! It would be much easier for us to blast our enemy with a curse. But Jesus said not to do that.

If anyone understood this principle, it was Jesus, who did only good and was murdered for it! While Jesus was hanging in agony and suffering on the cross, He blessed His tormentors and said, "Father forgive them, for they do not know what they do" (Luke 23:34). The last thing He did before ascending to heaven was to lift His hands and bless His disciples: "And He led them out as far as Bethany, and He lifted up His hands, and blessed them" (Luke 24:50). Romans 12:17–21 sheds more light on blessings:

> Repay no one evil for evil. Have regard for good things in the sight of all men. If it is possible, as much as depends on you, live peaceably with all men. Beloved, do not avenge yourselves, but rather give place to wrath; for it is written, "Vengeance is Mine, I will repay," says the Lord. Therefore "If your enemy is hungry, feed him; If he is thirsty, give him a drink; For in so doing you will heap coals of fire on his head." Do not be overcome by evil, but overcome evil with good.

From the examples we have seen in the above quotes from the Bible, it is evident that the blessing is the supernatural power of God imparted by spoken words over another person. This means that you and I can speak blessings over our sons and daughters and our spouse, and even our entire extended family. We have the authority through our words, to not only

67

bind the work of the enemy in our lives, but also to release upon our family God's blessing in every area of their lives.

When we release blessings over our family and ourselves, we are taking a step beyond binding the enemy. Satan thought your house was his house, so he took up residence there. When we *reverse the curse* and pronounce a blessing on ourselves and our family, we are *spoiling* his house. In Matthew 12:29, Jesus says, "Or how can one enter a strong man's house and plunder his goods, unless he first binds the strong man? And then he will plunder his house."

Once you speak this spiritual blessing, (being the spiritual authority God has established over your household) it cannot be reversed. Remember the Old Testament account of Jacob, who through deception received the blessing that rightly belonged to his brother Esau? Once their father, Isaac, gave that blessing, he (Isaac) could do nothing to reverse it, even though Jacob deceitfully attained it.

> Then Isaac trembled exceedingly, and said, "Who? Where is the one who hunted game and brought it to me? I ate all of it before you came, and I have blessed him—and indeed he shall be blessed."
>
> When Esau heard the words of his father, he cried with an exceedingly great and bitter cry, and said to his father, "Bless me—me also, O my father!"
>
> But he said, "Your brother came with deceit and has taken away your blessing."
>
> —GENESIS 27:33–35

As an heir to the Abrahamic covenant and promises,

you and your family can be blessed, and once you speak that blessing over your family, nothing can be done to reverse it—*except disobedience or sin.* Short of that, nothing—no force in hell and no force on earth—will be able to stop or reverse that blessing. The force of heaven backs you up—praise be to God!

You can pray the following powerful prayer of blessing at any time over yourself and members of your family. Always pray aloud:

> The Lord bless you and keep you; the Lord make His face shine upon you, and be gracious to you. The Lord lift up His countenance upon you, and give you peace.
>
> —NUMBERS 6:24–26

Chapter Twelve

Entrapments That Open the Door to Strongholds

N THIS CHAPTER WE WILL EXPOUND ON SEVERAL areas of disobedience that can open the door to the enemy. Following are some of the snares, traps and pitfalls to avoid.

1. *Preaching another gospel or your acceptance of it*

Galatians 1:9 declares, "As we have said before, so now I say again, if anyone preaches any other gospel to you than what you have received, let him be *accursed*" (emphasis added). God did not make hundreds of different religions and cults. Religion is man's way to get to God. God desires a relationship with us. There is only one way to have that relationship— through His son Jesus, as we see in John 14:6: "Jesus said to him, 'I am the way, the truth, and the life. No one comes to the Father except through Me.'"

I'm not saying that you should not be associated with a church, but make sure the church you are associated with, or a member of, is one that believes and practices the entire teachings of the Bible and not just certain select portions. Being a part of a church fellowship is stressed in Hebrews 10:24–25: "And let us consider one another in order to stir up love and good works, *not forsaking the assembling of ourselves together,* as is the manner of some, but exhorting one another, and so much the more as you see the Day approaching" (emphasis added).

Christianity has changed the world, but, unfortunately, the spirit of antichrist is also changing the world. There are many churches here in our country today that are about as far away from the true gospel as a church can be, with hate messages, New Age theories, permissiveness and watered-down gospels. If you are a Christian who does not know what the Bible says and are not grounded and rooted in it, you are especially vulnerable.

2. *Trusting in the flesh instead of God*

Jeremiah 17:5 tells what happens when we trust human strength: "Cursed is the man who trusts in man and makes flesh his strength, whose heart departs from the Lord." It goes on in verses 7–8 to give a beautiful picture of the man who trusts in God: "Blessed is the man who trusts in the Lord, and whose hope is the Lord. For he shall be like a tree planted by the waters, which spreads out its roots by the river, and will not fear when heat comes; but its leaf will be green, and will not be anxious in the year of drought, nor will cease from yielding fruit."

3. *Not loving God*

Deuteronomy 6:5 proclaims, "You shall love the Lord your God with all your heart, with all your soul, and with all your strength." In the New Testament,

1 Corinthians 16:22 we read, "If anyone does not love the Lord Jesus Christ, let him be *accursed* . . . " (emphasis added).

If you love Him, you will honor Him. If you honor Him, you will obey Him. And if you obey Him, you will serve Him. God desires first and foremost that you love Him. What you do for Him should be done out of the deep love you have in your heart for Him, not because you feel guilty or because someone else expects you to do certain things. Your motives are important to God! They can be hidden from your fellowman, but not from God.

4. *Idolatry*

Exodus 20:3 says, "You shall have no other gods before Me." Anything we worship and esteem higher than God is considered an idol. Idols are not just "carved images," as some people may think. Idols are anything that can get between you and worshiping, serving and trusting in God. Do you worship a "religion," people (saints), figures, relics, etc.? Do you worship your spouse, children, job, automobiles, money, material things? Many people don't think of that as idolatry. But does your love for your spouse, your job, hobbies or anything else ever come between you and God? Only you can answer that. Matthew 6:33 says, "But seek first the kingdom of God and His righteousness, and all these things shall be added to you."

Constantly manipulating, controlling, compulsively trying to arrange all the outcomes, or controlling another person, (rather than trusting in God)—these are also forms of idolatry, bordering on witchcraft.

If you love the approval of man more than the

approval of God, that is idolatry. We read about that in John 12:43 when it speaks of the Pharisees, "for they loved the praise of men more than the praise of God." This scripture is referring to the rulers in Jesus' day who believed in Jesus but, because of the Pharisees, did not confess Him for fear that they would be put out of the synagogue.

5. Not tithing
Malachi 3:8–9 says, "Will a man rob God? Yet you have robbed Me! But you say, 'In what way have we robbed You?' In tithes and offerings. You are cursed with a curse, for you have robbed Me, even this whole nation."

Many in the church are under a curse—not tithing brings them under it! We are to give a tenth of our income to God as a tithe, and anything over and above that is an offering. God also tells us He loves a cheerful giver, and I believe the spirit in which we give is just as important as the fact that we give it. The scripture goes on to say in Malachi 3:10 regarding tithing, "'And try Me now in this,' says the Lord of hosts, 'if I will not open for you the windows of heaven and pour out for you such blessing that there will not be room enough to receive it.'"

6. Abortion
Abortion is murder, and the shedding of innocent blood will be very costly in the final judgment day unless a person has confessed it as murder and asked God for forgiveness. Exodus 20:13 says: "You shall not murder." Unwanted pregnancies happen every day, and millions of innocent lives are taken every year because of these unwanted pregnancies. Some statistics say as many as one in every three pregnancies

73

ends in abortion.

Immoral activities always carry a price tag. There can be guilt and/or shame attached that lasts for years and years, leading to psychological and physical problems because of the tearing that takes place—taking a life, when only God has the authority to do that. Deep depression or even insanity can follow an abortion. Once a woman has an abortion, she is under a curse. The next abortion becomes easier, enforcing strongholds deeper into one's life. God is the only one who can give life and take life. I do not believe that God will allow the killing of innocent babies to continue much longer before a horrible judgment takes place.

Once this sin has been confessed to God as murder, He will forgive both the father and mother of the aborted baby. A woman who has truly repented of having an abortion should forgive herself as well; she does not have to continue to live with shame or guilt. Any party involved in the decision to murder through abortion should also repent and ask forgiveness.

7. Covetousness

The tenth commandment says, "You shall not covet . . . " (Exod. 20:17). Covetousness is desiring what belongs to someone else. Lust, gambling and greed can all be manifestations of covetousness. They bring on a curse if they are allowed to continue and become a stronghold in a person's life. Jesus taught the people, "Beware, and be on your guard against every form of greed; for not even when one has an abundance does his life consist of his possessions" (Luke 12:15, NAS).

Gambler's Anonymous says the increase in homelessness is directly related to the increase in gambling.

74

The curse is the addiction—lives can be ruined and families destroyed, all at the expense of the one who is addicted. Greed always causes a problem. First Timothy 6:9–10 says, "But those who desire to be rich fall into temptation and a snare, and into many foolish and harmful lusts which drown men in destruction and perdition. For the love of money is a root of all kinds of evil." It is not money itself, but the love of money that is the problem.

Covetousness can be more than just coveting someone else's material things or being greedy for gain. It can also be manifested by lusting for or coveting another person's spouse, which often results in adultery, broken marriages, troubled children and so on. It always starts with a single thought of lust or covetousness.

8. *Laziness and refusing correction can bring poverty and shame*

Proverbs 13:18 says, "Poverty and shame will come to him who disdains correction, but he who regards a rebuke will be honored." Proverbs 19:15 says, "Laziness casts one into a deep sleep, and an idle person will suffer hunger." Again, in the New Testament, "If anyone will not work, neither shall he eat" (2 Thess. 3:10).

Poverty can also come from mismanagement of finances or from an obsession for material things that leads to overspending, or living beyond one's means. Some people have an addiction to shopping, and in our society today it is easier than ever to use credit cards to charge for purchases way beyond our means of paying for these items.

Poverty or bankruptcy can also be the result of

uncontrollable addictions such as gambling, alcohol or drugs. Poverty often tends to run in families—but this cycle can be broken right now and does not have to continue in your family!

9. *Envy or Jealousy*

These two emotions will almost always cause visible strife unless they are carefully concealed. Even then they will come out sooner or later. James tells us, "If ye have bitter envying and strife in your hearts, glory not, and lie not against the truth. This wisdom descendeth not from above, but is earthly, sensual, devilish. For where envying and strife is, there is confusion and every evil work" (James 3:14–16, KJV).

You may have great spiritual wisdom and knowledge. But if there is bitterness in your home, strife in your heart, envy at your workplace—don't think you are spiritual at all. You are under delusion. When James speaks of strife and bitterness, he is also talking about arguing and faultfinding. And anyone who holds on to the bitterness resulting from the strife opens his heart to demonic strongholds.

10. *Pride*

Proverbs 16:5 says, "Everyone proud in heart is an abomination to the Lord; though they join forces, none will go unpunished." It goes on in verse 18 to say, "Pride goes before destruction, and a haughty spirit before a fall." Pride is the opposite of humility and has been the downfall of many Christians. It was also the downfall of Lucifer (Satan) as we see in the account of his fall. Isaiah 14:12–15 describes that fall:

> How you are fallen from heaven, O Lucifer, son
> of the morning! How you are cut down to the

ground, you who weakened the nations! For you have said in your heart: "I will ascend into heaven, I will exalt my throne above the stars of God; I will also sit on the mount of the congregation on the farthest sides of the north; I will ascend above the heights of the clouds, I will be like the Most High." Yet you shall be brought down to Sheol, to the lowest depths of the Pit.

This recorded event is an example to show us what can happen when our self-will, pride and arrogance get in the way. Pride is manifested in many different ways and often comes about when people come into material wealth, success or fame and find it hard to maintain a proper sense of humility. Sometimes knowledge puffs a person up or the "pride of life." First John 2:15–16 says:

Do not love the world or the things in the world. If anyone loves the world, the love of the Father is not in him. For all that is in the world—the lust of the flesh, the lust of the eyes, and the pride of life—is not of the Father but is of the world.

Many people today think they are part of a superior race and their feeling of superiority causes them to hate people of other races and cultures. Supremacist groups abound today, and even some churches promote hate and discrimination. Some well-meaning Christians can be filled with self-righteousness and have "holier-than-thou" attitudes that are a big turn-off to the rest of the world. James 4:6 says, " . . . God resists the proud, but gives grace to the humble." Proverbs 11:2 declares, "When pride comes, then comes shame; but with the humble is wisdom."

11. *Children dishonoring parents*

Children who rebel against their parents bring a curse on themselves and that curse can be passed on to future generations.

> Honor (esteem and value as precious) your father and your mother—this is the first commandment with a promise—that all may be well with you and that you may live long on the earth.
> —EPHESIANS 6:2–3, AMP

Honoring your mother and father doesn't end at a certain age. It doesn't matter if you are a teenager living at home, married living with your parents or married living apart from your parents. Parents are not always perfect, and we may not always agree with them, or like their behavior, as it may be. We are not to take advantage of them in any way, at any age.

I have seen people take extreme advantage of their ailing or aged parents, making sure they get the best of the inheritance, taking control of money and property, not caring what the parent's wishes are for the other children. Their excuses were, "I'm the oldest, I deserve more, or I took care of them more than the others, and because of that, I deserve more. Besides, all the other siblings need it less than I do, or don't need it at all."

It's not about being the oldest or the neediest or about which of the children took care of Mother or Dad the most! It's about honoring the wishes of the parent! There is a dire price to pay for dishonoring parents! The cost is high and a curse may be in operation for one who disobeys or dishonors his parents. Repentance is in order and deliverance may be needed.

Proverbs 30:11 says, "There is a generation that curses its father and does not bless its mother." I have heard parents say to their children, "You just wait until you have children; they'll treat you the same as you are treating us and probably worse." Two wrongs do not make it right. They are dishonoring a parent by words or actions, and the parent is putting into motion a curse on the child. Both bring a curse; both are wrong!

Young people using controlling behavior to manipulate and control their parents are dishonoring them. Using is abusing your parent, and it is no different than lying or stealing from them. It is disobedience and rebellion—it will bring on a curse. Wonder why things are not going right in your life when you seem to be doing all the right things? It may be time to do some real soul searching and survey your present and past attitudes toward your parents and your treatment of them! Do your children have negative attitudes towards you because you are not treating your parents with honor and respect?

Proverbs 20:20 declares, "Whoever curses his father or his mother, his lamp will be put out in deep darkness." This is a profound statement and should be heeded at all costs. The Hebrew word "darkness" means misery, destruction, sorrow, death!

If you rebel against your parents, you may think you are getting away with what you are doing, but you aren't. It doesn't matter whether you agree with what they're saying; if you curse them, you'll also bring a curse upon yourself, and possibly pass it on to your children. (Obviously, if your parents tell you to do something that is contrary to the Bible, you should not do it.)

God desires to bless His children, but how can He when they are living in sin? Our God is a jealous God—sin and righteousness cannot both prevail in our lives at the same time—one will always prevail over the other!

Chapter Thirteen

Why the Secret of the Occult?

HERE IS SOMETHING MYSTERIOUS ABOUT THE occult. I believe that the mystery or intrigue of the occult is one of the main reasons why millions of people are involved or becoming involved in occult practices today. Many are born into families where one or more family members are already involved in occult practice. Still others get involved simply to be accepted. Today, witchcraft, or Wicca, is even touted as a "positive but misunderstood alternative religion." Most people do not understand the underlying force or danger behind the occult. In this chapter, the following questions will be answered:

1. What is the occult?
2. Why is the occult so secretive, and what is its purpose?
3. Where can it lead a person?
4. Why is the occult dangerous?

5. What is the power behind the occult, and from whom does that power come?
6. Why isn't the hidden agenda of the occult openly revealed?
7. How does the occult conflict with God's plan for mankind?

There is a certain excitement and curiosity that causes people to dabble in various aspects of occult practices. The occult is yet another tool Satan uses to get an entirely unsuspecting victim to sin. The lure is power—power to know future things, power to cast spells, etc. But this power comes with a hefty price tag called a curse. God does not forbid good things—only evil things that will cause a person to be destroyed. To be involved in the occult is to practice evil! The occult stronghold is caused in two ways:

1. Personal involvement or choice
2. Passed on from previous generation by mother, father, grandparent or other relative

The occult lures a person by any number of methods and accepts anyone. Most participants blindly give themselves to this mysterious evil. The evil hidden beneath the disguise, the true purposes of the occult and the real forces behind them are never revealed until it's too late. Converts are sucked into the whirlpool in a downward spiral that leads to ruin, despair and depression. Their lives are under dark forces of evil. They become captives to a host of other strongholds that are connected to the occult, such as lust, perversion, deception, rebellion, drugs and the list goes on.

Occult practices have infected all levels of our

society from the inner-city slums to the high office of the president of the United States. Several years ago the wife of the president was consulting astrologers to get advice pertaining to the governing of our country, and high-level decisions were being made from that advice. Occult practices are still used in some high government places.

Over the years, millions of people have become desensitized to the dangers of the occult. It has become an accepted, non-threatening vehicle that influences every level of our society. It is accepted by millions daily who base their plans and activities on the advice of horoscopes in almost every newspaper in the world.

TV's infomercials sell their brand of occult practices in the form of so-called "real psychics," who can, supposedly, tell you about yourself, your circumstances and your wonderful future! They advertise that your life will be changed for the better because you called them and they have the answers. This is a multi-million dollar business—Satan's business—to get you hooked by a stronghold of divination and familiar spirits. Remember, familiar spirits know almost everything about you, but they do not know the future—only God knows the future.

When you believe or trust in these evil forces that portray themselves as good witches, palm readers or happy-go-lucky psychic readers, you believe in information that comes from an evil source. This information does not come cheap—ask anyone who has dialed the so-called psychic reading come-along numbers. Before you realize it, your call has been switched from an "800" number to a very expensive

"900" number to trained personnel who will gladly give you an earful of anything you want to hear—everything but the truth.

A recent newspaper article spoke out boldly against psychics, astrologers, palm readers and crystal-ball gazers. The article was titled "Trusting in crystal balls . . . can sometimes cost more than disappointment." The writer pointed out that even though predictions of future events may sound harmless and fun, they can lead to serious consequences. He gave an example of a woman in Chicago who withdrew $122,000 from her bank account to pay a fortune teller who had promised to remove an evil curse from her. Another woman, when told by a psychic that she was barren, suffered needless fear and anxiety for years before she eventually had children.

If you believe in psychics or fortune tellers, as these two women did, not only do you run the risk of losing your money or suffering needless fear and anxiety, but, even worse, you open yourself up to deceiving spirits.

The word *occult* means "secret or hidden." Now let's see what the secret is and from whom it is hidden. First we must understand this basic principle:

There are two forces that oppose each other—good and evil.

God is good. Satan is evil. The occult is hidden because the forces behind it are evil and do not want to be exposed as dangerous to the human race. God has always given us good things openly to help the human race and to expose the dangers of evil. God has revealed His will and His plan for mankind. He desires that none should perish but that all should come to the saving knowledge of Jesus Christ, as we see in John 3:16, "For God so loved the world that He gave His only begotten Son, that whoever believes in Him should not perish but have everlasting life."

The occult is not fully comprehended by most people; as a matter of fact, it is understood only by a chosen few. Who are they chosen by, and what is the source of their hidden power? Satan and demonic forces of evil, of course! These chosen few who have mastered occult practices lead their various understudies through them, and subsequently lead thousands of unsuspecting people into the mysterious realms of the unknown. For very good reasons, they keep their converts literally in the dark in evil deception.

In a recent article from *Charisma* magazine, a former psychic who at one time was high priestess of a local coven told about her experience when she decided to turn away from her occult practice. She told *Charisma*, "It started out as a happy, healing journey, but it turned out to be just the opposite in the end. There are levels. The deeper you go, the greater the bondage."

She decided to renounce witchcraft when she was pressured to embrace necromancy—the practice of communing with the dead. But walking away from witchcraft wasn't easy. After leaving, she was plagued by demonic nightmares and threats from her former friends, such as, "You can run but you can't hide." Today, stronger in her Christian faith and keenly aware that there are many caught like she was, she runs a ministry for witches who want to find a way out of the web.

TV shows such as *"Sabrina: The Teenage Witch"*

and "*Charmed,*" as well as movies such as *Practical Magic* and *The Craft* have made the occult appear both fashionable and fun. A popular game called "Magic: The Gathering" is played by an estimated six million people, many of them preteens and teens, who are taught to cast spells and summon spirits.

Sadly, according to one recent survey, witchcraft is the number one interest of teenage girls! Just as disturbing is the information disclosed this summer that the Pentagon allows Wiccans to worship openly on military bases.

The Harry Potter book series, which have been on *The New York Times* and *USA Today* bestseller lists for months, also deal with the occult. A pastor at Evangel Assembly of God in Ohio was recently quoted as saying, "In the books, you find animal sacrifices, threats of human sacrifices, witchcraft, wizardry and divination." Another parent said, "[They] have a serious tone of death, hate, lack of respect and sheer evil." Even though some concerned parents have influenced principals and teachers to ban the books in their schools, the books are still being read by teachers at many other schools around our nation today.

Pokémon is the latest fad for children ages four to fourteen, and this invasion into our children's lives is part of another troubling trend today. It debuted in Japan in 1996, and in 1998 was introduced in the United States. Nintendo has spent twenty million dollars on publicity, and sales have now reached the one-billion-dollar mark. The game has 151 characters, and the main goal is to recruit and train these monsters to fight one another, using psychic powers, channelers and white magic. Some of the characters then grow or evolve into more powerful creatures. It is a quest for control and dominance.

Most Christian parents agree that Pokémon fosters greed, combativeness, competition and obsessiveness—traits that show up in the children who are involved almost immediately. The noticeable result in the children is fighting, a marked change in personality and other anti-social behavior.

Pokémon is heavily influenced by Eastern religions, such as Shinto and Buddhism, which are predominant in Japanese culture. These belief systems are not compatible with Christianity.

Drugs and certain kinds of music can open the mind to the occult and the demonic forces. Have you ever seen screaming, incoherent crowds of young people at a concert waving the satanic hand gesture wildly over their heads? Whether they know it or not, they are open to numerous kinds of strongholds. Some of the things mentioned heretofore should be red flags. Once people are hooked by the intrigue of any form of the occult, they become blinded by deception, and the reality of what they are involved in is never truly understood.

Occult practice has been around for a very long time. I often remind people, "All occult roads lead to Curseville—no exceptions." A person can be set free from this curse only through true repentance and deliverance.

Many people are afraid of the occult's mysterious, dark powers; some even believe that the forces of evil are stronger than the power of God. There is nothing further from the truth—God is all-powerful! In stark contrast to the occult, God's Word is openly available to all who desire the truth and will call upon Him. God's wisdom, understanding, knowledge and power are available to all who will believe and trust in Jesus.

In Jeremiah 33:3, the word of the Lord came to him, "Call to Me, and I will answer you, and show you great and mighty things, which you do not know." This direct line to God is free of charge, never busy and doesn't have voice mail. He is available twenty-four hours a day, seven days a week. He is never out to lunch, on vacation or off for a holiday. Ephesians 1:17–18 shows how God will give us revelation knowledge if we diligently seek Him:

> That the God of our Lord Jesus Christ, the Father of glory, may give to you the spirit of wisdom and revelation in the knowledge of Him, the eyes of your understanding being enlightened; that you may know what is the hope of His calling, what are the riches of the glory of His inheritance in the saints.

The apostle Paul is praying that God will give His people insight into mysteries and secrets that only a deep and intimate knowledge of Christ can bring.

Let's look at the account of the deliverance of Israel from bondage in Egypt. Moses was a Hebrew, raised as an Egyptian, educated as a son of Pharaoh. Moses knew the customs and practices of that world system. While on the run and in the wilderness, he had an encounter with God that changed his life and, subsequently, the lives of millions of others.

Moses was called and instructed to deliver the suffering people of Israel out of bondage. When Moses returned to Egypt, God caused Pharaoh to fear Moses.

Pharaoh actually looked at Moses as though he were God, as we see in Exodus 7:1, "So the Lord said to Moses: 'See, I have made you as God to Pharaoh, and Aaron your brother shall be your prophet.'"

God commanded Moses to have Aaron, his prophet, perform a miracle before Pharaoh by throwing down his staff and having it become a serpent (vv. 9–10). But why a serpent and not a tiger or a lion? Because a serpent was the very thing that represented Satan and was cursed in the Garden of Eden. The magicians likewise, cast down their staffs, and their staffs also became serpents.

Moses and Aaron didn't jump back in fear and say, "Oh my, what are we going to do? They have more serpents than we do!" No, they stood confident, believing in God's power, as Moses' serpent swallowed up the replicas produced by the sorcerers. The magicians were able to duplicate the feat, but they could not replicate the miracle. I believe the message God was sending to the world ruler, Pharaoh, and his servants was this: "Look, I used the serpent I created to destroy all your serpents, proving my power is greater than all your combined efforts. You and your serpents will always be under my control."

The sorcerers/magicians would again challenge the power of the man of God. When Moses turned the water into blood, the magicians likewise did the same (Exod. 7:20–22). If the magicians had been smarter they would not have duplicated the feat. But no, they had to prove they could create more blood, causing more problems than they already had!

The Lord later instructed Moses to cause frogs to come, and they literally covered the land. The

Egyptian magicians hadn't learned from their previous experiences, so they called up more frogs, making the land doubly full of frogs (Exod. 8:5–7). Why didn't the magicians reverse the plagues? Because they did not have the power to overcome God's power! Throughout history, evil has reared its ugly head in one way or another. Its objective is still to control and/or destroy mankind; it has not changed. The forces of evil will continually challenge the power of God. It is spiritual warfare.

When the children of Israel were delivered from Egypt, and they were set free, many of them continued to practice abominations to God they learned earlier while in captivity.

> *In the same way, many Christians continue to carry baggage from their worldly walk after they are born again.*

If you are carrying spiritual baggage, strongholds or sin habits, God wants you to receive deliverance and come out from under the bondage that is controlling you. To start on the road to freedom, let's recognize some of the practices that can put you in bondage.

God banned eight practices that people frequently used to try to determine future events or future actions:

1. Witchcraft
2. Soothsaying (possibly referring to conjuring up spirits or practicing astrology)
3. Interpreting omens
4. Sorcery—using magic formulas or incantations

5. Casting spells
6. Consulting a medium
7. Consulting a spiritist (one who often works with or is connected to a medium)
8. Attempting to communicate with the dead

God has never lifted that ban—it still applies today. God never reveals the future through any occult practice!

Today, the occult is practiced by many different groups as well, including the following:

1. Fortunetellers
2. Psychics
3. Palm readers
4. Witches/warlocks
5. Stargazers/astrologers
6. Zodiac followers (those who rely on horoscopes)
7. Amateur hypnotists
8. Enchanters
9. White and black magic practitioners

If you can identify any of these areas in your life or know of anyone in past generations who has been involved in any occult practice, then a stronghold may be in operation. Acts 19:18–19 tells how new believers in Ephesus renounced their past occult involvement:

> And many who had believed came confessing and telling their deeds. Also, many of those who had practiced magic brought their books together and burned them in the sight of all. And they counted up the value of them, and it totaled fifty thousand pieces of silver.

CERTAIN TYPES OF
JEWELRY CAN ATTRACT EVIL SPIRITS

CHRISTIANS WEAR THESE THINGS INNOCENTLY; NEVERTHELESS, they can attract evil spirits, and, if you are a Christian, I'm sure that's the last thing you would want to do.

There is a cross with a circle on top of it, and some people think this cross represents Jesus. Nothing could be further from the truth. It's called an *ankh,* and it was an emblem of life to the ancient Egyptians. The circle or loop symbolized the uterus of a woman, and the stem represented the male sex organ. The bar symbolized the union of the two. Wearing the ankh meant you worshipped Ra, the Egyptian sun god and chief deity. Sex orgies were a part of the ritual of sun-god worship.

Scarab jewelry is very popular and looks perfectly innocent. It has an image of a beetle on it that is cut into a stone or gem. This black, winged dung beetle was held sacred by the ancient Egyptians as a symbol of re-incarnation (resurrection).

Another piece of jewelry you may see people wearing is what looks like a broken cross. People who join satanic cults are usually given a cross of Christ and told to turn it upside down and break the cross bars to show rejection of Jesus.

You may have seen many people wearing the Italian horn around their necks. I remember wanting to get one several times, but something kept me from it. I didn't know at the time, but this symbol can have several meanings. Some believe it wards off an Italian curse; and others use it to say that Satan blesses or looks after your finances. (It is also sometimes called a leprechaun staff.)

To be free from occult strongholds, you must first remove any and all tangible occult items now in your possession, whether in your home, in your car, at your office or any place they may be.

This includes items such as the jewelry mentioned above, Ouija boards, troll dolls, tarot cards, horoscopes, astrology material, crystal balls, or items pertaining to black or white magic, etc. Any magazines or publications associated with these items should also be included.

These items need to be destroyed, just as the Ephesians did as recorded in the Book of Acts. Then you must renounce any of these activities as sin hidden in your life and receive forgiveness and freedom from them.

First John 4:4 declares, "You are of God, little children, and have overcome them, because He who is in you is greater than he who is in the world." It is God's mighty power in you that will make you an overcomer. Remember, God is aware of what you are facing. He understands you, sympathizes with your weaknesses and loves you unconditionally. He does not want you to allow any evil forces to keep you in bondage and fear.

Chapter Fourteen

Dangers Behind the Music

USIC HAS BEEN AN INTEGRAL PART OF MANY cultures for thousands of years, and each culture's music has a distinct type of rhythm beats and blends of various instruments and sounds. Music is good and has been given to us as a gift. It is for our enjoyment, entertainment and praise and worship of God.

Psalm 150, without doubt, is the clearest direction to us for using not only our voices, but also instruments of various kinds to magnify our praise and worship to the Lord:

Praise the Lord!
Praise God in His sanctuary;
Praise Him in His mighty firmament!
Praise Him for His mighty acts;
Praise Him according to His excellent greatness!
Praise Him with the sound of the trumpet;
Praise Him with the lute and harp!

Praise Him with the timbrel and dance;
Praise Him with stringed instruments and flutes!
Praise Him with loud cymbals;
Praise Him with clashing cymbals!
Let everything that has breath praise the Lord.
Praise the Lord!

Music is intertwined into every fabric of our society and is the language of nations around the world. By its very nature, it speaks volumes. Music, like no other communication vehicle, can stir up a wide range of emotions and memories, from euphoria to sadness. It can even give us a strong sense of well-being. Various studies have shown that music helps people physically and emotionally. Listening and participating in music and/or singing can lower blood pressure and increase production of endorphins, the body's natural pain reliever.

In addition to its emotional and physical effects, music that is used in worship also has a spiritual impact. I have witnessed praise and worship services during which people were saved, healed and delivered from the bondage of Satan, and no one had to preach or lay hands on anyone! Praise motivates God to move.

Israel used music to defeat armies that were made up of Moabites, Ammonites and Edomites bent on Israel's destruction (2 Chron. 20:1–24). God instructed Jehoshaphat to have the musicians lead the army in loud singing and praising, which moved God to act on their behalf. The enemy was defeated!

Anointed music, praise and worship sends dismay and terror into the enemy's camp, for the battle belongs to the Lord (v. 15), not us. God has not

changed—He is the same yesterday, today and forever. He acted for them, and He will act for us.

However, we still have an enemy who is bent on our
destruction. One of his most potent weapons is aimed
at our children. They call it music—most parents call
it garbage. There should be no doubt that its composer
is the master of deception, Satan. In these last days, he
has intensified his efforts to control, destroy and corrupt by using music that manipulates and that often
results in violence. Music is, by far, one of the most
effective enchantments he uses to further his cause.

Music took a dramatic turn in the mid-fifties and
early sixties when rock 'n' roll was introduced.
Whether it was as bad as some contended it to be at
the time is debatable, but I do believe it was used as a
catalyst for a more dangerous kind of music. As
people became more desensitized, a radical, more
intensified form of music was being introduced. By
the early seventies, the assault was full steam ahead,
and it was starting to have a profound effect on our
young people, with results we are just now beginning
to comprehend. America has spawned some of the
most enduring types of music known anywhere, but,
unfortunately, America has also given birth to some
of the most radical types of music as well.

This radical music was not designed for main-
stream music lovers but was targeted at our children.
It has had a more profound and dangerous effect on
the minds and spirits of our young people than any
other kind of music in history. Heavy metal (appro-
priately known as underground music) is its name. It
is still too radical for many radio and MTV stations,
but the question is for how long.

Most of this music is performed by groups rather than individuals. The group members share the same moral makeup and degenerate ideals, which makes them compatible and unified in their quest to influence and pervert their listeners with words of hate, rebellion, drugs, sex, suicide, bondage and chaos. Our young people are easily swayed by the unnatural influences of these "culture-shock" bands. The band members appear to be driven and motivated by self to satisfy their own lust and perversion, and to corrupt all who will follow them.

These bands are sophisticated. Seemingly by magic they can induce and produce a euphoria that can boggle the mind, turning listeners into an unmanageable, unpredictable and dangerous mob. This underground movement has produced such groups as Anthrax, Def Leppard, Kiss, Guns & Roses, Marilyn Manson, Ozzy Ozbourne and many more who are satanically influenced, and, indeed, some will admit it. We cannot ignore their existence and the effect they have on our young people.

One group that stands out the most is known as Metallica, the masters of heavy metal. They have been around for about twenty years, although they have somewhat cleaned up their personal appearance even wearing short hair. They are still a force and leader in heavy metal, packing stadiums full, with standing room only for screaming, frantic, out-of-control young people. They have somehow charmed this young generation with rebellious, loud and distorted music that produces head bangers and body slammers who go into a maddening frenzy, causing injury and, sometimes, death.

The band Metallica prides itself on its lack of morals, rebellion and alienation. They have openly admitted in television interviews that they thrive on negative and belligerent attitudes and want to pass on their values to their listeners via their music or antics. They appear to be self-willed and obsessed with perverse behavior that satisfies their hunger for anything and everything. Their type of music has a magical, hypnotic effect that captivates its listeners, inducing them to every form of violence, sexual perversion, suicide and destruction of moral values. These and many other heavy metal bands frequently use subliminal messages and backward masking to promote their form of gospel.

There is no doubt that the music has deafening sound effects and exceptionally fast rhythm and beat. The air is charged with an explosion of physically-felt negative energy that often leads to violence and lawlessness. In this atmosphere of sight, sound and emotionally-driven energy, there is an open invitation to minds and souls to be influenced and controlled by demonic forces. Millions across the world unwittingly become controlled in this way to one degree or another.

Perestroika began over ten years ago in Russia. This allowed Christians to openly evangelize, but at the same time it opened the door to the gospel of heavy metal. Metallica was allowed to perform in Russia before some five hundred thousand young people. Mayhem and violence broke out, and in this crowd of half a million, perversion, rage and anger prevailed. No amount of police action could control them. When it was over, two hundred women reported being forcibly raped, not including those who did not report it. Thirteen people were killed. All the while, the crowd lifted their satanic hand gesture, as they do at all heavy metal concerts. Violence became the order of the day. Do you still think music has no effect on minds, or that these bands are innocent and their music non-harmful? Think again. During that one concert in Russia, many lives were changed and some lost forever. These out-of-control incidents barely received mention in the media, let alone condemnation for promoting violence of every kind.

It is time for parents to wake up and take a firm stand with tough love.

Get involved. Know what your children listen to, where they are going and with whom they are associating. Your child's life may depend on your caring. If you are afraid you're going to lose them if you intervene in their lives, guess what? If you don't intervene, guess who will? It's never too late.

There is a battle being waged in this arena for the control and bondage of our children, and even some adults. Satan will always use an avenue, a means that appears good or harmless on the surface, to perpetuate his evil. Satan can appear in many shapes and disguises, even as an angel of light, to lure us to abandon our faith in Christ or to confuse our convictions. He is the author of confusion. His main goal is to deceive God's creation, and if certain kinds of music facilitate that process, he will continue to use them effectively—if we let him!

Chapter Fifteen

Strongholds of Fear

OR GOD HAS NOT GIVEN US A SPIRIT OF FEAR, but of power and of love and of a sound mind" (2 Tim. 1:7).

There are many, many kinds of fear—about four pages' worth if you were to research it at your local library. But none of them are godly, nor do they come from God. There are many evil spirits Satan uses to make people miserable, but I believe that fear is the primary one.

The word *fear* usually has a negative connotation, but some fear is good. A healthy fear (precaution) will generally keep one from making dumb mistakes or doing wrong things, such as driving 120 miles per hour on a mountain road or walking out into the middle of a busy street. This kind of healthy precaution may keep a person alive. On the opposite end of the spectrum are the excitement junkies who are looking for a thrill a minute and will do almost anything to get a rush. They are the ones whose lack of healthy fear or precaution makes the headlines because their stunts get them hurt, get someone else hurt or even get someone killed. They disregard the healthy fear mechanism that keeps most people in line and safe.

The only other healthy fears are fear of the Lord and fear of the consequences of sin. Matthew 10:28 says, "And do not fear those who kill the body but cannot kill the soul. But rather fear Him who is able to destroy both soul and body in hell."

Fear is one of the devil's favorite weapons. He uses it to intimidate, discourage and torment us. He often uses fear in ways that keep us from doing the right thing or help us to continue doing the wrong thing. Fear comes in all forms and shapes and is used in a variety of ways. There are a host of problems connected with strongholds of fear, and each of these strongholds is manifested in various ways. In this chapter, we will expose some of these unfounded fears!

Superstitions and charms

There are many superstitions that are passed down from generation to generation that are not based on truth. For example, people say, "Don't walk under a ladder; don't step on the cracks in a sidewalk; if you break a mirror, it will mean seven years of bad luck; or it's a bad omen if a black cat crosses in front of you."

Webster's definition of superstition is, "Any belief based on fear or ignorance that is not in accord with known science or with what is considered true and rational, especially such as charms and omens."

For thousands of years people have been using charms to bring good luck or ward off evil. Charms are not unique to any one culture. In fact, most cultures of the world have them. A recent factoid on TV said that according to a recent *Ladies' Home Journal* poll, 75 percent of Americans say they carry some kind of good-luck charm. A charm is based on superstition and fear, not on fact. When people have a lack of faith or no faith in God, they resort to something such as a charm, as a point of contact, something tangible that they can feel or touch to help them quell their fears.

It is well known that superstitions are deeply rooted and difficult for people to put out of their lives. I have heard many reasons why people put their faith in good-luck charms. I have also heard people say they don't believe in charms yet refuse to remove them from their homes or from around their neck or wrist.

A charm is a myth, and the variety of charms worn by people all over the world is staggering. Millions of people put their faith and confidence in something made of plastic, stone, metal, or wood, maybe carved or imprinted, of every description, shape and size. Many of these images are also worshiped and revered as gods within their homes and places of worship all over the world.

Four-leaf clovers, shark's teeth, animal parts, trolls, statues of persons or things—none of these have any special or magical powers. They cannot hear you or see you, nor can they feel. Having them in your possession will not profit you in any way. The only ones who profit from them are the ones making them and selling them. It is superstition that propagates the continued use of inanimate objects.

What about the rabbit foot? Thousands of key chains made from rabbit feet are sold every year. People will rub the little furry foot and say, "This is my good-luck charm!" If the rabbit foot was so lucky, why did the rabbit who had four of them lose it? If four feet didn't bring him any luck, what makes the owner of one foot think he is going to have better luck than the rabbit?

What about religious objects?

Religions around the world all have religious symbols that identify their particular religion and faith. People of certain religions actually worship the things they have created with their hands, such as images made from stone or wood, representing animals, or people that once lived.

God forbids all worship of anything other than Himself. In Exodus 20:4, He declares, "You shall not make for yourself a carved image—any likeness of anything that is in heaven above, or that is in the earth beneath, or that is in the water under the earth." This means anything—charms, gods, symbols, etc. The punishment for doing so is severe.

I came from a Catholic background before I became a born-again Christian and have a thorough knowledge of the beliefs of Roman Catholicism. Some of my close friends are Catholic, and from time to time we talk about various aspects of the differences in our religious beliefs.

About twenty-five years ago there was a shake-up in the Catholic church when the Vatican announced that they were discarding (discounting as myths) many of the patron saints who were believed to have had an impact on the church. The real shocker came when the patron saint of travel was cut from the role of sainthood. St. Christopher now became a myth. This presented a dilemma, since so many people had previously put their faith in this figurative person. All these people for years had medals or images that they wore or had in their homes or automobiles. They had trusted in this figure that turned out to be a myth and had no power to protect a person. Many still refuse to let go of this myth, still wearing this figure as a medal, as though it would help them.

Myths die hard and are dangerous because people put their trust in them, and not in God. People are afraid to put them aside! If you put your trust in God instead of charms, images, idols or things, He will remove all your fears and protect you.

Anxiety and worry

Worry is a major problem that plagues many people of the world needlessly. It's a fact that we live in perilous times. Many people have an uneasiness that something is "in the air." There is an expectancy of some great change that's about to take place. People are looking for change, longing for peace, security and prosperity. But what they see is a world where the problems seem to be becoming more complicated and magnified all the time. Financial markets are collapsing. Governments around the world are finding it more and more difficult to cope with and suppress all the current outbreaks of violence and wars. According to Matthew 24:3–13, Jesus said the world would become more wicked, violent and full of trouble before His return:

> Now as He sat on the Mount of Olives, the disciples came to Him privately, saying, "Tell us, when will these things be? And what will be the sign of Your coming, and of the end of the age?"
>
> And Jesus answered and said to them: "Take heed that no one deceives you. For many will come in My name, saying, 'I am the Christ,' and

will deceive many. And you will hear of wars and rumors of wars. See that you are not troubled; for all these things must come to pass, but the end is not yet. For nation will rise against nation, and kingdom against kingdom. And there will be famines, pestilences, and earthquakes in various places. All these are the beginning of sorrows.

Then they will deliver you up to tribulation and kill you, and you will be hated by all nations for My name's sake. And then many will be offended, will betray one another, and will hate one another. Then many false prophets will rise up and deceive many. And because lawlessness will abound, the love of many will grow cold. But he who endures to the end shall be saved."

A lot of worrying or panic about all the chaos in the world today will not change these facts. Worry is the fear of what might happen, or the fear of future events over which we have absolutely no control. We can change events by our actions, but wringing our hands, pacing the floors, looking out the door every minute for fear of the thing you are concerned about will not change the outcome. In fact, the only thing worrying will do is break you down physically and emotionally and keep you from being effective and at peace.

Excessive worry produces anxiety, stress and fatigue, which weakens the immune system. This sets up the scenario for disease to attack the vital organs of the body, such as the heart (heart attack), stomach (stomach ulcers), nervous system (nervous conditions), cells (cancers) to name a few. It has even been reported recently that worry actually destroys brain cells.

Fear of the unknown

We have all been through stressful situations in our lives at one time or another. If you have children of your own, you know that there is a tendency to worry a bit about whom they are with and what they are doing. Often we may have that fear of the unknown. I've heard many people say their children or husband/wife "worries them sick." Jesus said in Matthew 6:27, "Which of you by worrying can add one cubit to his stature?" In other words, you can no more change your height than you can change something by worrying about it. If you trust in God, then you know that doubt and unbelief is sin. God does not want you to worry because He knows that the enemy is the source of worry (fear). The Bible tells us what to do in Philippians 4:6–7:

> "Be anxious for nothing, but in everything by prayer and supplication, with thanksgiving, let your requests be made known to God; and the peace of God, which surpasses all understanding, will guard your hearts and minds through Christ Jesus."

Worry is the opposite of contentment, and God wants us to be content at all times, even in the face of adverse circumstances, knowing that He alone has all things under His control. It's more important than ever in these days of uncertainty to draw closer to God. If you will yield completely to Him through prayer and the reading of His Word, He will quell your fears and fill you with the peace and security that you will need in the coming days when people all around you may very likely be filled with panic.

Fear of saying no

If we say no, we worry that we might not be liked or get the approval of those around us. As a result, many people actually make up a lie to keep from having to say no. Or we say yes when our hearts say no and then later resent ourselves for having done something we really did not want to do, did not have the time to do or did not have the resources to accomplish. Often, we just go with the flow to keep from making waves, and we let others set our priorities for us. Or we let someone else lay a guilt trip on us and we buy into it.

The fear of saying no is linked to the fear of rejection (insecurity) and an inability to be assertive. We can eliminate ninety percent of our stress—before it occurs—just by being assertive. Stress produces anger, fear, anxiety, pain and rejection. It just makes sense that if we learn to be assertive (not passive and not aggressive), we will eliminate a lot of fear and anxiety from our lives.

Fear of rejection

There are many reasons given by psychologists as to why people have a fear of rejection, and I don't profess to know all the reasons. I do know this is a common fear, and many people appear to have been born with it. It is manifested by a strong need to be liked by others or have the approval of others. This fear causes a multitude of sins.

For example, we live in a permissive society, where many parents are afraid of saying no to their children because they are afraid that the children will dislike or reject them. The truth is that when parents say no, the children will usually respect them more as authority figures who care and love them enough not to compromise their own convictions and standards just to allow the children to have their way.

Another example is in our churches' pulpits. Pastors are often afraid of being rejected by their congregations or not being liked anymore. They may be afraid of losing members or losing money. Because of this fear, they often choose to sugarcoat their words in order not to offend or step on toes. They try to please everyone all the time (when even God can't do that). Or, it may be they refuse to take a hard-line stance on an issue and instead prefer what they perceive to be the safer, middle-of-the-road stance. Or, because of a fear of confrontation, they avoid the issue altogether, hoping it will go away.

I believe this is one of the reasons why our whole society has become more permissive. We now find ourselves as Christians having to be reactive, when being proactive would have prevented some of the problems we face in our world today. Hindsight is always 20/20!

A third example of the fear of rejection is the incredible peer pressure in the world today, especially for our children. Their fears of not being accepted will cause them to partake in alcohol, drugs or sex at an early age for fear of being rejected or fear of being alone or, worse yet, being ridiculed or persecuted.

A fourth example is in a relationship between a man and a woman. Many people stay in relationships that are wrong for them because either or both are insecure, afraid of being alone or afraid of rejection.

Don't scare your children

The presence of fear can be felt in hospitals, doctor and dentist offices, and even in some homes. Again, it is due to a fear of the unknown. No matter how these places are decorated or what kind of music is playing, there is often an element of fear. A stronghold of fear can grip a person to such an extent that they dread hospitals or visiting the dentist or doctor so much they refuse to return for checkups or follow-up work.

Without knowing what a hospital or doctor's office is, children will often sense fear as soon as they enter the premises. They are very vulnerable and very sensitive to the presence of fear, whether it is actual or sensed from parents or others on the premises. They often balk with tears in their eyes or tantrums when going into some of these places. Consideration for the child's fear should be addressed in a prayerful and positive way before going to a place where fear is likely to attack them.

The fears of a child can last through a lifetime and be passed on to future generations. Your child's fears are real to him or her and must be treated as real. The boogeyman is real to a child (even to some adults). To tell a child that the boogeyman will get them if they do the wrong thing is to place a stronghold of fear on them, possibly for life—and they will probably do the same thing to their children.

When I was growing up, my older brothers and sisters used to tell me the boogeyman was behind trees, under my bed, in the closet or in the basement. After all these years, I can still remember the fears that were instilled in my young life. I was afraid to open a closet for fear that something would pop out at me. When I *had* to open a closet, you can be sure I kept my distance, always on guard, ready to run in the event anything moved in that closet.

As a young boy, my running skills were excellent and improved greatly at night when I had to walk home in the dark. In fact, the only time I walked was when I was with someone. If I was alone, I was running. If there was a boogeyman behind a tree, he had to be fast if he wanted to catch me!

The basement was another story. I was told the boogeyman was everywhere in that basement. It took years before I could go in the basement without fear. Finally, at about the age of thirteen, I said, "Enough is enough." I made it a point to turn off the lights while in the basement and walked up the stairs as slow as I could, not looking behind, never to fear again. I made up my mind that fear would never attack me again in the same way. I no longer feared dangling my hands and feet off the bed (the boogeyman wasn't there anymore in my mind either).

Halloween, too, is a time when fear is perpetuated needlessly. It boggles my mind how this holiday that has its roots in pagan rituals became so popular and commercialized. Many people think it is innocent fun. Fortunately, most churches have recognized how this holiday provides nothing in accordance with our Christian beliefs and are now providing alternative "harvest celebrations" rather than celebrating demons, ghosts and witches. There is no such thing as a good witch. Parents and siblings, if you use the boogeyman or anything else to put fear in your children's minds, you may be helping to put unnecessary fear in their lives that may last for generations.

Paranoia and irrational fears

Satan plays on our fears and magnifies them in our minds. He is the author of confusion and will cause us to jump to conclusions rather than using the "sound mind" given to us by God to get to all the facts before we speak. At the other end of the spectrum, Satan can blind the healthy fear (normal precaution) that keeps us from self-destruction by convincing us we are invincible.

Fear brings in other connected strongholds, and one can literally be imprisoned within his or her own body to the point of becoming paralyzed and not able to function normally. Fears, when magnified, can become paranoia, which is extreme and irrational. If it is allowed to get a stronghold on one's life, it can cause a mental disorder characterized by systemized delusions of grandeur or persecution. This paranoia will create a tendency toward excessive or irrational suspiciousness and distrustfulness of others. This condition can be very dangerous, because the fears are actually playing tricks on one's mind at this point. Know this: the power of the Holy Spirit can set you free no matter how extreme or irrational your fears may be.

Fear can enter years before it becomes manifested. My mother was a victim of fear that had a connected stronghold. When she was fifteen years old she came to America by ship from Italy. The great expanse of open water with no land in sight, and the continuous waves caused her to fear for her life. Great fear came upon her to the point that it would affect her for over fifty-five years.

When I was growing up, whenever my mother came under stress and anxiety, she would have uncontrollable convulsions. Medically, there was no reason for her to have these bouts. She would throw herself down and flop like a fish out of water, completely out of control. My father was a big man, and he could barely restrain her as she flailed in his arms, even with the help of my older brothers. He would ask one of us to get him a glass of water with which he would splash her. After ten or fifteen minutes, she would get up and return to normal as if nothing had happened. Each time it happened, the rest of us were fairly shaken up. Her doctor just said it was "her nerves," and we believed him. But no matter what pills she took, the same manifestations were there. We grew up with it and accepted it as a way of life. But that wasn't the way it was supposed to be.

In 1981 my mother asked me to come over to her home. When I arrived, she asked me to sit down and said, "I want what you have. I want to really know Jesus." I was shocked and a little startled. Since my born-again experience in 1971, I had tried many times to bring my mother to a place to accept Jesus in her life, with no success. This time it was no effort. God had set it up. He had placed a desire in her heart, and I was the one who would be privileged to birth my mother into the kingdom of heaven through prayer and leading her to accept Jesus.

As I lead my mother into repentance and acceptance of Jesus, tears were flowing from both our eyes. The joy was evident on both of us. But as soon as she accepted and confessed Jesus as Lord, that ugly, convulsing thing that had been plaguing her for fifty-five years rose up. My first thought was, *"Where is the glass of water? I need to splash her with water like I saw my father do so many times."* The Lord spoke to my spirit and said "No water this time. Call that spirit of fear out of her and bind it up—now!" I said, "OK." I called it out and bound it up. It came out, and Mom calmed down. That was the last convulsion she ever had—and she lived for eighteen more years. Praise God! If God could do it for her, He can do it for you.

Fear of evil and violence

Fear can become manifested because of wicked-ness/evil in men's hearts. Matthew 24:37–38 says:

> "But as the days of Noah were, so also will the coming of the Son of Man be. For as in the days before the flood, they were eating and drinking, marrying and giving in marriage, until the day that Noah entered the ark."

Jesus was saying to us that it was business as usual, that they were eating, drinking and being merry, yet all around them evil existed. They became desensitized to the conditions around them. "But as the days of Noah were" is described in Genesis 6:5:

> Then the Lord saw that the wickedness of man was great in the earth, and that every intent of the thoughts of his heart was only evil continually.

Where there is evil, violence is not far behind. We live in a world that is filled with evil of all sorts, a time where good (truth) is viewed as evil, and evil is viewed as good. Violence may be viewed by most as evil, yet the world is captivated and intrigued by it. World news media report violence all over the world (rape, murder, mutilation) twenty-four hours a day, seven days a week. Millions consume this steady diet of mayhem through newspapers and television. There seems to be a never-ending appetite for violence, except when it happens close to home. Then there is much condemnation and outrage and people asking why someone doesn't do something about all the violence and crime. Once it hits home, it's too late.

Today, in nations all over the world, people are fighting and mutilating each other, and this violence is growing faster than any nation or group of nations can keep up with it. The slaughter and mutilation of innocent people by warring factions around the world fulfills a two-fold purpose: 1) control by killing, and 2) control by instilling fear.

When the news is reported, the expressions on faces everywhere show fear and anguish. Each war had its atrocities and those who were to be feared. Many nations have had infamous organizations whose purpose was to instill fear, such as the Gestapo in Germany, the KGB in Russia and the Vietcong in Vietnam. Watching film clips of the activities of these groups causes people to fear, and understandably so. Violence will cause just about anyone to fear!

Genesis 6:11–13, says:

> The earth also was corrupt before God, and the earth was filled with violence. So God looked upon the earth, and indeed it was corrupt; for all flesh had corrupted their way on the earth. And God said to Noah, "The end of all flesh has come before Me, for the earth is filled with violence through *them;* and behold, I will destroy *them* with the earth."
>
> —EMPHASIS ADDED

The word *them* is mentioned two times in the above verse. Who is God referring to here as *them,* and how did they corrupt the earth? Let's go back to Genesis 6:4:

> There were giants on the earth in those days,

and also afterward, when the sons of God came
in to the daughters of men and they bore children to them. Those were the mighty men who
were of old, men of renown.

It indicates here that the "them" were the sons of
God. These were the same sons of God mentioned in
Job 1:6 and Job 2:1–2. These sons of God may actually have been fallen angels who did not keep their
proper domain as indicated in Jude 6–7. Second Peter
2:4–9 indicates they corrupted the cities of Sodom
and Gomorrah and caused them to be destroyed.
They were probably a special class of angels all by
themselves. We could infer this from Job 2:1–2:

Again there was a day when the sons of God came
to present themselves before the Lord, and Satan
came also among them to present himself before
the Lord. And the Lord said to Satan, "From
where do you come?" So Satan answered the
Lord and said, "From going to and fro on the
earth, and from walking back and forth on it."

I believe the sons of God referred to were not mere
men. These sons of God, along with Satan, were
occasionally required to present themselves before
the Lord! Because these sons of God left their first
domain, they are today kept in chains of darkness.

Evil and violence were always present when God
destroyed a culture. Evil, violence and the effects of a
stronghold of violence fill the whole world today. We
live in a "culture-shock" world, filled with much rebellion and hate. All around us, people are killing their
co-workers in the workplace, children are killing
other children and teachers in schools, parents are

killing children and children are killing parents, all for no reason. Those committing the crimes often say they don't know why they did it or don't even remember committing the violent act. Most probably don't. Often, they show no remorse! The killing, raping, etc. are manifestations of a stronghold of violence and lawlessness in our world, and the results are more evident every day.

Hollywood has successfully desensitized film watchers to the point that almost nothing bothers them anymore, to the extreme point where mutilation and body parts being splattered all over the screen is what some people seem to want. If they didn't, they wouldn't continue to go to violent movies. The more one sees, the more desensitized one becomes, so the violence must be depicted in an even more graphic manner in order to have shock value.

Satan knows he has but a short time, so everyone is under attack from every imaginable direction, and this includes our children, as well.

In Revelation 12:12 we read, "Therefore rejoice, O heavens, and you who dwell in them! Woe to the inhabitants of the earth and the sea! For the devil has come down to you, having great wrath, because he knows that he has a short time." Violence is a curse, and anyone who enjoys committing violent acts or condones violence is under a curse. Keep away from it, don't permit it, and don't pass it on to your children.

Fear of persecution

Many people today lower the standard given to us

in the Bible for living a godly life, and therefore do not stand out as beacon lights to the rest of the world. They become fearful of what people might think of them, so either they become very introverted, or they act like those around them. They don't want pot shots taken at them because they wear the label of "Christian," so they become "private" Christians. Nowhere in the Bible does it say we are to be private Christians. If we are believers, we are commanded to proclaim the gospel of Jesus Christ, not try to hide it!

Second, there are those who take on the stance of being "flexible" Christians, bending the commandments a little in order to keep the heat off of them, acting a little (or a lot) like the world, so that they fit in.

In either case, fear is the culprit—fear of persecution, fear of not being liked, fear of rejection or fear of not fitting in.

The world perceives the private Christians, or those who don't walk by faith in their daily lives, as weak, religious people who are not motivated by their beliefs, except in the privacy of home or at church, almost ashamed of who they are as Christians.

The second type, the flexible Christians, who bend the rules and dabble in worldly things so they don't bring too much attention to themselves as Christians, are perceived by the world as hypocrites. They are seen as weak, indecisive or phony where spiritual matters are concerned. They usually have one type of behavior when they are in church and perhaps quite another type when they are out in the world. The uniform doesn't quite match up with the person inside.

Both private and flexible Christians are ineffective witnesses to the power of Christianity. Born-again Christians should not be surprised by persecution because it comes with the territory. In the early days, persecution is what made the church strong. After the ascension of Christ, persecution caused the church to be dispersed around the known world at that time and it helped the disciples become stronger. Since they were dispersed, they had to rely completely on the Lord. It was through the power of the Holy Spirit that they had the strength and courage to persevere in spite of tremendous adversity. Where would we be today if they had not persevered?

How comfortable and complacent we have become. Christians need to stand upright, unwavering, steadfast in their faith—and be proud of it! The Bible says in Mark 8:38, "For whoever is ashamed of Me and My words in this adulterous and sinful generation, of him the Son of Man also will be ashamed when He comes in the glory of His Father with the holy angels."

Many major churches and denominations never seem to suffer persecution. Is it because they have chosen the safe road? In 2 Timothy 3:12 the Bible says, "Yes, and *all* who desire to live godly in Christ Jesus *will* suffer persecution." If you don't have the courage to witness to others and share the undiluted, unadulterated, uncompromising word of God, it's unlikely you will hear the words "well done, good and faithful servant" from the Lord.

Religious Cults Seem to Have No Fear of Persecution

On many occasions, I have seen the disciples of various religious cults freely hand out information on street corners, in airports and almost any place where there is access to an open public. I've watched them in groups or "in twos" knocking on doors, proclaiming their form of the gospel, some being rejected, but never appearing to become discouraged by rejection. I had to ask myself why they seemed to have no fear of rejection.

I believe it is because they are not teaching the true gospel that Jesus Christ is the Son of God, lived on earth, died on the cross, was resurrected, ascended into heaven, and is coming again someday. Because their teaching is false, they are no threat to Satan's kingdom! Satan is the author of false religions; therefore, he wants to see people led away or kept in the chains of deception. And since Satan (not God) is the one who puts fear in and on a person, these people teaching their false religions do not have the fear of persecution. They are there earning their brownie points, believing all along that they can work their way into heaven.

There's only one problem with that philosophy. How many brownie points does it take to get into heaven? Theirs is an empty religion void of truth about the free gift of salvation provided through acceptance of Jesus Christ, the Son of God. This gift was given freely and was not based on our ability to earn it.

Christians, wake up! It is our duty to spread the true gospel of Jesus Christ. He will empower us by His Holy Spirit, and signs and wonders will accompany us as we go into the world. Mark 16:15–18 makes it clear in the scripture that follows:

> And He said to them, "Go into all the world and preach the gospel to every creature. He

who believes and is baptized will be saved; but he who does not believe will be condemned. And these signs will follow those who believe: In My name they will cast out demons; they will speak with new tongues; they will take up serpents; and if they drink anything deadly, it will by no means hurt them; they will lay hands on the sick, and they will recover."

This is not a suggestion. It is a command. This command was not given just to the twelve disciples, as some Christians mistakenly believe today. This command was given to all who believe and are baptized. This power is available to all Spirit-filled believers, whether you got filled with the Holy Spirit by an official "baptism in the Holy Spirit" or just got filled sitting at your kitchen table or in your car or wherever. The Holy Spirit has not changed, and that same power and authority is still available today for those "who believe."

There are many forms of religion but only one true gospel.

If a so-called church teaches anything other than the gospel of Jesus Christ, then it is a false religion— designed to deceive and destroy its followers. They have no hope! There is only one way—God's way. Millions are led down the wrong path when they do not follow the clear instructions given by Jesus Christ. Anyone who changes—takes away or adds to the gospel as it was given to us—is accursed. Paul the Apostle states in Galatians 1:9, "As we have said before, so now I say again, if anyone preaches any other gospel to you than what you have received, let him be accursed."

Fear of the Lord is healthy

Most of our fears keep us in bondage. God wants to deliver us from the bondage of unhealthy fears. The Bible clearly instructs us that we are to fear nothing— not another person, event or circumstances that we find ourselves in—nothing except God Himself. That fear is reverence of Him, respect for His power and fear of His judgment. Scripture describes the fear of the Lord this way:

- The fear of the Lord is clean, enduring forever (Ps. 19:9).
- The fear of the Lord is the beginning of wisdom (Ps. 111:10).
- The fear of man brings a snare, but whoever trusts in the Lord shall be safe (Prov. 29:25).

Fear is the opposite of faith

We have the power to control all our fears through faith in God and the power of the Holy Spirit. Fear is the opposite of faith, and Hebrews 11:6 tells us that without faith it is *impossible* to please God.

GOD'S PERFECT LOVE

FIRST JOHN 4:18 TELLS US, "THERE IS NO FEAR IN LOVE; but perfect love casts out fear, because fear involves torment. But he who fears has not been made perfect in love." What does that mean? That means when you have truly learned to abide in the perfect love of God, you will not have the torment that fear brings into your life! Jesus is the manifestation of perfect love. Once you truly realize that nothing can separate you from God's love, you will gain complete victory over fear!

Chapter Sixteen

The Curse
of Sexual Sins

OD COMES DOWN HARDER ON SEXUAL SINS THAN
any other kind of sin. The Bible deals
extensively with sexual sins.

In Deuteronomy 27:20–23 we see the following:

- *Cursed* is the man who sleeps with his father's
  wife, for he dishonors his father's bed. Then all
  the people shall say, "Amen!"
- *Cursed* is the man who has sexual relations
  with any animal. Then all the people shall say,
  "Amen!"
- *Cursed* is the man who sleeps with his sister,
  the daughter of his father or the daughter of his
  mother (incest). Then all the people shall say,
  "Amen!"
- *Cursed* is the man who sleeps with his mother-
  in-law. Then all the people shall say, "Amen!"

—NIV, EMPHASIS ADDED

In Leviticus 18:22–25, we see further clear instructions:

You shall not lie with a male as with a woman. It is an abomination. Nor shall you mate with any animal, to defile yourself with it. Nor shall any woman stand before an animal to mate with it. It is perversion.

Do not defile yourselves with any of these things; for by all these the nations are defiled, which I am casting out before you. For the land is defiled; therefore I visit the punishment of its iniquity upon it, and the land vomits out its inhabitants.

The Levitical law governing sexual conduct was given to the redeemed of the Old Testament and applies as well to the redeemed of the New Testament. The judgment (wrath) of God was rendered against cities/nations whose people conducted themselves in all forms of sexual immorality. They paid the ultimate price—death and total destruction! God destroyed some cities Himself, and in some He ordered the armies of Israel to kill every man, woman and child, as well as the animals, and then to burn them with fire. Some people may question how this could possibly happen if God is so full of goodness and mercy.

I believe, there are two main reasons:

1. *The inhabitants of those cities were involved in every kind of idolatrous practice.* God had delivered Israel from Egypt and did not want them to mingle or mix with other inhabitants of the land who worshiped other gods or with those who were controlled by many strongholds and all sorts of evil workings.

2. *They were involved in gross sexual perversion.*

Modern-day archaeologists have discovered ruins from some of these ancient cities that the Bible describes as having been completely destroyed. Their finds are astonishing in that not only did they find the ruins and determine how these cities were destroyed, but they have found bone fragments that survived all these years (and the fire itself). These bones showed advanced stages of syphilis, which is transmitted by sexual intercourse and, if left untreated, will damage brain tissue, blood vessels or other organs. I don't believe God wanted this disease, or any other like it, to contaminate the children of Israel.

The modern-day plague that continues to spread around the world is AIDS (HIV). Some areas of the world carry a staggering number of HIV carriers—about one in four people in some places. The cost in human lives is escalating, and the cost in dollars is soaring as well, with no end in sight. Intravenous drug addiction, sexual immorality and promiscuity are taking their toll in this situation. Everyone wants a cure, but the best cure is prevention—abstinence from sex outside of marriage, and only then with a spouse of the opposite sex whom you trust as a safe partner. People in the high-risk category who don't want abstinence and want to continue playing with deadly fire will pay the price! The price of sin is high, as we see in Romans 6:23: "For the wages of sin is death . . . "

How did this evil immorality begin, and what purpose does it serve?

It all started in the Garden of Eden when Satan deceived Eve, and Adam fell by willingly sinning.

Deception is the key to Satan's success. It is Satan who deceives mankind, and man is willing to allow it by disobedience to God's laws and by believing Satan's lies. The more of Satan's lies you believe, the more you will find yourself struggling in life. Since God did not want us to be a bunch of robots, man was created with a free will and the right to choose. All of us are free moral agents who have a conscience designed to help us choose between right and wrong. Those choices we make, whether right or wrong, pave the road on our walk through life.

In our society, sexual sins are out of control, prompted and perpetuated by billboards, magazines, books, television, movies, the Internet and so on. Curiosity often causes an "urge to experiment" that outweighs good sound judgment, and when that happens, self-control is no longer being exercised.

In the 1960s the slogan was "make love, not war." Free sex was the beginning of Satan's new, accelerated plan to conquer the souls and minds of men and women through sexual strongholds. It continues to accelerate without slowing down a bit. Just standing in line at the grocery store, one cannot help but be bombarded by magazine covers designed to encourage lust and sexual fantasies.

Satan's ability to deceive, manipulate and control has not diminished since the temptation of Eve in the Garden of Eden. In fact, it's much more sophisticated and widespread now. Remember the serpent in the garden? The serpent lent itself to Satan, and the end result was that it was cursed to crawl on its belly all of its life. Satan, as well as all his cohorts, were already cursed before the Garden of Eden.

After the Garden of Eden, in Genesis 6, we see how

the whole earth was filled with evil, wicked people who were open to any and all forms of corruption. These people wanted more, and Satan knew how to pervert the good things that God gave to mankind. If mankind wants it, they will get it—in the form of adultery, fornication, lesbianism, homosexuality, sex with animals and pornography. Pornography rates high on the list of strongholds, and the results are uncontrolled lust, perversion and uncleanness. Many families carry these strongholds from generation to generation, and uncontrolled lust prevails.

In Genesis 6:5, the Bible says, "Then the Lord saw that the wickedness of man was great in the earth, and that every intent of the thoughts of his heart was only evil continually." Men's hearts were filled with every imaginable form of wickedness. They had free will, were curious and had a lot of satanic influence! The women of that era were apparently also willing to experiment with their sexuality.

Genesis 6:2 says "that the sons of God saw the daughters of men, that they were beautiful; and they took wives for themselves of all whom they chose." We see how the women's association with the sons of God made the women vulnerable. These mortal women were selected by the supernatural sons of God because of the women's free will and their desire to experiment. In that way, the women defiled themselves.

It's no different today. Satan's demonic forces are still as strong and more than willing to help a person become more wicked and under his control. Jeremiah 17:9–10 declares:

> The heart is deceitful above all things and desperately wicked; who can know it? I, the Lord

search the heart, I test the mind, even to give every man according to his ways, according to the fruit of his doings.

God destroyed an entire civilization in Noah's day because men's hearts were polluted and the evil strongholds that controlled them continually became worse. It was always man's choice. In that day, only eight people found grace in God's sight. They trusted in the words of the Lord and were saved when they entered the ark of safety, Noah's ark. I believe the day will soon come when the faithful believers will be taken out of this polluted, evil world into the safety of the "ark" of Jesus. It's up to each of us to be ready when that day comes.

The Bible is full of dire warnings telling us the severe penalty of sexual immorality, yet it is mostly ignored as an old-fashioned idea, not to be taken seriously in this day and age. *Nothing could be further from the truth!*

It is the sexual sins of mankind that are so dangerous. Aside from man's survival instinct, the sex drive is probably the most powerful instinct. Ironically, our survival may largely depend on our control of our sexual instincts and appetites.

Sex is also man's greatest weakness. Men and women, rich and poor, great and ordinary, preacher and layman have all succumbed to the allure and power of sex! The power of sex has perverted, destroyed and ruined more individuals, churches and marriages than anything else. It will bring down a king and a peasant alike. There is no other natural power like it on earth.

Once the stronghold of sexual sin has latched on to a person, only God and His power can free one from it. It is through these sexual strongholds that Satan controls and manipulates his captives. Once control is established, these sexual curses die hard! Everything attached to unlawful sex can become a stronghold.

Remember that God comes down harder on sexual sins than any other sin!

Why? There are two ways that sexual strongholds can develop: 1) through the loins of the mind and 2) through the loins of the body.

We read in 1 Peter 1:13, "Therefore *gird up the loins of your mind,* be sober, and rest your hope fully upon the grace that is to be brought to you at the revelation of Jesus Christ" (emphasis added). To gird the loins of our mind simply means to guard the entrance to our thought processes. Again, in Genesis 6:5, we read, " . . . that every intent of the thoughts of his [man's] heart was only evil continually." Therefore, we need to protect our minds from evil thoughts.

The mind absorbs the garbage we put in it, and it's very difficult to take the garbage out once it enters. Watching pornography or triple-X-rated movies and looking at filthy magazines is garbage in. Some people think pornography is harmless, but it is very dangerous. After the photograph is displayed before the eyes, it is developed quickly in the darkroom of the mind where it stays in the subconscious. Even when you are not thinking about it, pornography will pop into your mind.

Pornography has victims and is not to be considered an innocent adult pastime. Both those who watch and those who perform are cursed. The curse is the addiction. A strong foothold is being established as one allows the conduit of the mind to open up, and the thought to pass through it into the spirit. Ephesians 6:11–14 says:

> Put on the whole armor of God, that you may be able to stand against the wiles of the devil. For we do not wrestle against flesh and blood, but against principalities, against powers, against the rulers of the darkness of this age, against spiritual hosts of wickedness in the heavenly places. Therefore take up the whole armor of God, that you may be able to withstand in the evil day, and having done all, to stand. Stand therefore, *having girded your waist with truth . . .*
>
> —EMPHASIS ADDED

The first thing we are told to do when putting on the armor of God is to gird our waists. The waist area referred to here is the loin, or sexual reproductive area of our body.

First Peter talks about protecting the loins of our minds, but here in Ephesians it speaks literally of protecting the loins of our bodies. Why? The loin area is our reproductive area. It is the conduit (channel) by which bodily fluid passes from one person to another. It is well known that diseases may be transmitted in this manner.

Even beyond that, the joining of two is a spiritual as well as a natural act. Any demonic entities that are present can pass from one person to the other, or they can join forces, establishing strongholds and becoming part and parcel of that other person. They can eventually control that person, and possibly future generations. The sexual intercourse might be a free-will exchange, maybe just a one-night stand, but the end result could be a world of iniquity that goes on and on, perhaps even to your children's children.

When you have sex with someone, you open yourself to receive anything (and everything) that your partner may have received from anyone (and everyone) with whom he or she has had sex and vice versa.

All these entities can move and exchange positions through individuals like an enormous underground network of tunnels, running through lives, affecting and controlling the thoughts and actions of their captives.

Uncleanness is the result. Galatians 5:19 states, "Now the works of the flesh are evident, which are: adultery, fornication, uncleanness, lewdness . . . " Unclean spirits are connected to any sexual activity outside of marriage, or any illicit sexual activity, and can take control of one or both persons involved. The apostle Paul speaks of these activities in Romans 1:21–32 below:

> Because, although they knew God, they did not glorify Him as God, nor were thankful, but became futile in their thoughts, and their foolish hearts were darkened. Professing to be wise, they became fools, and changed the glory of the incorruptible God into an image made like corruptible man—and birds and four-footed animals and creeping things.
>
> Therefore God also *gave them up to uncleanness*, in the lusts of their hearts, to dishonor their bodies among themselves, who exchanged

the truth of God for the lie, and worshiped and served the creature rather than the Creator, who is blessed forever. Amen.

For this reason God *gave them up to vile passions.* For even their women exchanged the natural use for what is against nature. Likewise also the men, leaving the natural use of the woman, burned in their lust for one another, men with men committing what is shameful, and receiving in themselves the penalty of their error which was due.

And even as they did not like to retain God in their knowledge, God *gave them over to a debased mind,* to do those things which are not fitting; being filled with all unrighteousness, sexual immorality, wickedness, covetousness, maliciousness; full of envy, murder, strife, deceit, evil-mindedness; they are whisperers, backbiters, haters of God, violent, proud, boasters, inventors of evil things, disobedient to parents, undis-cerning, untrustworthy, unloving, unforgiving, unmerciful; who, knowing the righteous judg-ment of God, that those who practice such things are deserving of death, not only do the same but also approve of those who practice them.

—EMPHASIS ADDED

In verse 24 it says, "God gave them up to unclean-ness." The word *unclean* here is from the Greek word *ak-ath´-ar-tos,* which means "demonic." In verse 28 it says, "God gave them over to a debased mind." Here in these scriptures, Paul is referring to the vile pas-sions of all illicit sexual sins, especially lesbianism and homosexuality. The fact that God gave them up and gave them over means He seared their consciences on the matter, and, at that point, they no longer knew the difference between right and wrong.

In 1 Corinthians 6:9–10, the Bible declares:

> Do you not know that the unrighteous will not inherit the kingdom of God? Do not be deceived. Neither fornicators, nor idolaters, nor adulterers, nor homosexuals, nor sodomites, nor thieves, nor covetous, nor drunkards, nor revilers, nor extortioners will inherit the kingdom of God.

Homosexuals, pederasts (those who practice anal intercourse, especially with boys) who violate catamites (boys kept by those who practice pederasty) and sodomites are among those who will not inherit the kingdom of God. Why? Because they are full of unclean spirits.

How did these unclean spirits get in?

1. They may have been passed from previous generations through spiritual heredity.
2. They may have entered by way of another person who was involved with someone who was involved with someone else who came into contact with someone who had a homosexual or lesbian spirit. They can move to a receptive host and spread like wildfire. Any illicit sexual activity can result in any kind of spirit exchange. *No person is meant to be a homosexual!* It is either passed on or acquired through illicit sex.
3. Participation in homosexual acts of any kind can open the door to unclean spirits. If a person thinks he is not a homosexual because he is not the one performing the sex act, that

is a false assumption. Whether you are "pitching or catching," you are still playing a most dangerous game. Your chances of being infected are very high!

4. Thought processes (fantasizing) about the idea of a same-sex partner can open the door through the loins (or channel) of your mind. Most activity of any kind usually begins with a thought about it first.

5. A child's experimentation with sex may open the door to unclean spirits. Children experiment with sex the same as they experiment with many other activities.

6. Pornography is another way that opens the door that may allow access to the participant or viewer.

Many people today try to convince us that homosexuality is normal and that this kind of behavior should be completely accepted as an alternative lifestyle, without bias. They march for gay rights, and many believe homosexual couples should have all the rights that heterosexual (straight) couples have, including getting married and raising children together.

Homosexuality is on the rise and it is spreading at an accelerated rate and no one seems to know why. So the answer from many religious leaders seems to be acceptance and tolerance. Sadly, our federal government has not only tolerated and accepted this lifestyle, but also has embraced it. Many people, even Christians, are believing a lie.

I have had interviews with a number of gay men who openly have shared their views, values and concerns. One of their biggest fears is the disproportionate number of homosexuals with HIV (which causes AIDS). Yet few seem willing to change their lifestyle because they believe the lie—that their lifestyle is normal, something with which they have been born and something over which they have no control! Many of them have been married previously and some have children. Most are open with their families about their sexual preference. Surprisingly, however, most say they would not want their children to have the same lifestyle.

Nearly all interviewed conceded they began to experiment and participate between ages thirteen and sixteen. Many reported molestation from another male (often a family member) as early as four or five years old. However, they rarely make the connection between the fact that they experimented (or were molested) and the fact that they are now homosexual.

Bisexuality and prostitution are also contributing to the rampant spread of homosexuality! I am sure that many people who are promiscuous are probably not even aware that some of their sexual partners have been bisexual. How could you know for sure? Even if you asked that question, the answer might not be honest. If you are promiscuous, you are not only open to undesirable, sexually-transmitted diseases, but also all kinds of perverse spirits.

God calls homosexuality/lesbianism an abomination. He even destroyed Sodom and Gomorrah completely, all because of the evil sexual perversion and homosexuality that had totally corrupted the inhabitants of these two cities. This story from Genesis 19:1–29 follows:

> Now the two angels came to Sodom in the evening, and Lot was sitting in the gate of Sodom. When Lot saw them, he rose to meet

them, and he bowed himself with his face toward the ground. And he said, "Here now, my lords, please turn in to your servant's house and spend the night, and wash your feet; then you may rise early and go on your way."

And they said, "No but we will spend the night in the open square." But he insisted strongly; so they turned in to him and entered his house. Then he made them a feast, and baked unleavened bread, and they ate.

Now before they lay down, the men of the city, the men of Sodom, both old and young, all the people from every quarter, surrounded the house. And they called to Lot and said to him, "Where are the men who came to you tonight? Bring them out to us that we may know them carnally [sexually]."

So Lot went out to them through the doorway, shut the door behind him, and said, "Please, my brethren, do not do so wickedly! See now, I have two daughters who have not known a man; please, let me bring them out to you, and you may do to them as you wish; only do nothing to these men, since this is the reason they have come under the shadow of my roof."

And they said, "Stand back!" Then they said, "This one came in to stay here, and he keeps acting as a judge; now we will deal worse with you than with them." So they pressed hard against the man Lot, and came near to break down the door. But the men reached out their hands and pulled Lot into the house with them, and shut the door. And they struck the men who were at the doorway of the house with blindness, both small and great, so that they became weary trying to find the door.

Then the men said to Lot, "Have you anyone else here? Son-in-law, your sons, your daughters, and whomever you have in the city—take them out of this place! For we will destroy this place, because the outcry against them has grown great before the face of the Lord, and the Lord has sent us to destroy it."

So Lot went out and spoke to his sons-in-law, who had married his daughters, and said, "Get up, get out of this place; for the Lord will destroy this city!" But to his sons-in-law he seemed to be joking.

When the morning dawned, the angels urged Lot to hurry, saying, "Arise, take your wife and your two daughters who are here, lest you be consumed in the punishment of the city." And while he lingered, the men took hold of his hand, his wife's hand, and the hands of his two daughters, the Lord being merciful to him, and they brought him out and set him outside the city. So it came to pass, when they had brought them outside, that he said, "Escape for your life! Do not look behind you nor stay anywhere in the plain. Escape to the mountains, lest you be destroyed."

Then Lot said to them, "Please, no, my lords! Indeed now, your servant has found favor in your sight, and you have increased your mercy which you have shown me by saving my life; but I cannot escape to the mountains, lest some evil overtake me and I die. See now, this city is near enough to flee to, and it is a little one; please let me escape there (is it not a little one?) and my soul shall live."

And he said to him, "See, I have favored you concerning this thing also, in that I will not overthrow this city for which you have spoken. Hurry, escape there. For I cannot do anything until you arrive there." Therefore the name of the city was called Zoar.

The sun had risen upon the earth when Lot entered Zoar. Then the Lord rained brimstone and fire on Sodom and Gomorrah, from the Lord out of the heavens. So He overthrew those cities, all the plain, all the inhabitants of the cities, and what grew on the ground.

But his wife looked back behind him, and she became a pillar of salt.

And Abraham went early in the morning to the place where he had stood before the Lord. Then he looked toward Sodom and Gomorrah, and toward all the land of the plain; and he saw, and behold, the smoke of the land which went up like the smoke of a furnace. And it came to pass, when God destroyed the cities of the plain, that God remembered Abraham, and sent Lot out of the midst of the overthrow, when He overthrew the cities in which Lot had dwelt.

God says sexual activities with a person of the same gender is abnormal, the work of the flesh, influenced by demons. But God, in His infinite mercy wants to save these people as well.

Homosexuality is not caused by a gene nor is it a person of the opposite sex trapped in the wrong body, as many would argue.

Homosexuality can be transmitted through unlawful and immoral sexual contact with a person of the same sex, through sexual activity with someone who is bisexual, or passed from parent to child through spiritual heredity. It is an unnatural act.

It is sin (a stronghold and a curse), and it is passed on and on and on. Men or women, boys or girls, who are raped or seduced by someone who has a homosexual spirit will often become influenced by this spirit themselves. That is not always the case, however. Sometimes this victim is used simply to pass these spirits on to another suitable candidate.

Homosexual spirits are driving their human "hosts" to push for legal (equal) rights of all sorts, including pursuing their agenda in schools as a moral and acceptable alternative lifestyle. The more successful they are, the greater the chances that the demon spirit of perverseness which causes homosexuality can be passed on and on even more quickly because of its acceptance. Nowhere in the Bible does God make provision for an alternative sexual lifestyle outside of marriage between a man and a woman.

Many homosexuals will pay another person for sexual services. The person who provides the service will also pay, but in a different way. The spiritual price tag is high and the curse will spread. Future generations will also pay the price of this sin, which the Bible clearly says is an "abomination to God."

In every culture and level of society, homosexuals and lesbians carry the same look and actions. Why? The same kind of spirit—Catamite, Effeminate, Sodomite—was passed on to another suitable candidate! There is a contamination and control of the body that can often be identified by apparent outward signs, because the demons are smug and haughty and pleased to have control. To be free of this difficult, controlling spirit, one must be purged (flushed out) and cleaned willingly by binding the demonic spirit, casting it out, and by faith applying the power of the cleansing blood of Jesus.

Unlawful sex of any kind may result in demonic influence or control. Sodom and Gomorrah were cursed with a devastating curse, as are other cities and nations who accept alternative lifestyles. Wholesale sin! God will not allow any society or nation to continue indefinitely but will give every opportunity to repent before judgment day.

The Internet may be the ultimate source of world information. This is the Information Age, and the technology is wonderful as well as useful, in varying degrees, for education, business, etc. But Satan has turned part of this technology into a highway full of snares, traps and pitfalls. Once again men and women, by choice and curiosity, have found the road of pornography available at the touch of a button. They can indulge in the privacy of their homes, no longer embarrassed by going to a video store or a XXX movie theatre. Now nearly every form of smut and perversion can be viewed without the rest of the world knowing about it. The stronghold of addiction to pornography can be played over and over again in one's mind and body. A sample is not enough for many because, once they taste, they may not be able to satisfy the driving force of uncontrolled lust that grips their souls.

These same spiritual forces that control a person through lust and perversion have a partner who works hand in hand with them. It's called rape, and it is violent and very dangerous. This is a powerful, violent spirit that drives the rapist to violate innocent victims. Rape and sodomy are not the work of the flesh totally. There is a spiritual force behind the rapist that is not interested in the sex act. The rapist may think it's his uncontrolled desire of sex that drives him, but, in most cases, it's not!

I read a recent newspaper article about Dennis Rabbitt, the man arrested and charged as the notorious "South Side Rapist" in St. Louis, Missouri. Rabbitt was quoted as having told the officers he had been possessed by a demon! This man was charged with approximately twenty-two attacks over a ten-year period.

Spiritual forces want to infect, impregnate and manifest themselves in their victims, with the goal of gaining a foothold that will give them access to more candidates. Spirits will go to great lengths to infiltrate and spread themselves through any means—much like a disease. The sexual organs are a conduit, or passageway they can use. Through the conduits of the mind and the body, whether by force, seduction or willful submission, one can receive everything unclean that the other person has to pass on and vice versa.

How does a person feel after they have been violated by rape? Only the person raped can truly know what it feels like. However, women almost always say they feel unclean, often taking many showers or baths afterwards, but still unable to stop feeling unclean. They say they feel dirty, shameful and violated, and many times develop low self-esteem and become consumed with bitterness. They may feel unwanted, outcast by society or even rejected by their own husbands. Divorce is often the result because either one or both are unable to cope with the devastating effects of the rape. Many turn to drugs, alcohol or even prostitution. Some commit suicide.

Matthew 8:28–32 says that even animals are so disturbed by demonic intrusion that they will resort to self-destruction:

> When He had come to the other side, to the country of the Gergesenes, there met Him two demon-possessed men, coming out of the tombs, exceedingly fierce, so that no one could pass that way. And suddenly they cried out, saying, "What have we to do with You, Jesus, You Son of God? Have You come here to torment us before the time?" Now a good way off from them there was a herd of many swine feeding. So the demons begged Him, saying, "If you cast us out, permit us to go away into the herd of swine." And He said to them, "Go." So when they had come out, they went into the herd of swine. And suddenly the whole herd of swine ran violently down the steep place into the sea, and perished in the water.

The swine did not want the unclean demonic spirits in them, so they committed suicide!

Many people under the influence of drugs or alcohol will do things they would not do any other time. They become bold and brave under the influence, making it easier for what's actually controlling them to do its dirty work. Violence, lust and perversion can all be triggered or enhanced by the effects of drugs and/or alcohol.

Sexual demons can also come on to a person while they are sleeping. They are even described in Webster's dictionary in the following way:

Incubus—"an evil spirit that lies on person(s) in their sleep; one that has sexual intercourse while they are sleeping." This spirit will take on the form of a man in order to have intercourse with women.

Succubus—"a demon that takes on a female form in order to have sexual intercourse with men while they are asleep."

These spirits can also work with members of the same sex and can produce seducing, whoredom, and perverse strongholds. In Deuteronomy 22:5 we read, "A woman shall not wear anything that pertains to a man, nor shall a man put on a woman's garment, for all who do so are an abomination to the Lord your God." Here we have an example of transvestites, another perverse situation.

Sexual strongholds are perpetuated by deceiving (demonic) spirits of perverseness and whoredoms. That spiritual veil of deception must be lifted before the person will be able to receive deliverance. Unfortunately, as we have stated throughout this book, any stronghold or curse may be passed on to the innocent victims of successive generations unless it is broken for good. God's awesome power and His unlimited grace are sufficient to deliver anyone who truly desires freedom from this (or any other) curse. I believe that person must truly want to be free, however, before it can happen.

Chapter Seventeen

Soul Ties

N THE AREAS OF SEXUAL MISCONDUCT, GOD'S WORD is true whether or not we choose to believe it and live by it. Four times the phrase, "And the two [or they] shall become one flesh" appears in God's Word—Genesis 2:24, Matthew 19:5–6, 1 Corinthians 6:16 and Ephesians 5:31. Any two who are joined together sexually become one flesh.

This oneness or *soul tie* is what was intended by God to help bond a marriage and make it strong. Unfortunately, we will become one with whomever we choose to become sexually intimate, whether one night, one week, one year or a lifetime. Adultery and fornication most probably will result in a soul tie. The apostle Paul makes it clear in 1 Corinthians 6:9–10 that adulterers and fornicators will not inherit the kingdom of God. Webster's defines fornication as "consensual sexual intercourse between two persons not married to each other."

Because there is an emotional bonding that takes place in a soul tie situation, there is also an emotional *tearing* that takes place when it is broken. That's why soul ties are so difficult to break—difficult, but not impossible!

For many people, a lifestyle of sexual immorality has taken its toll. They have left pieces of themselves all over the world. A man or woman has an affair, the affair ends, and years later, they are still thinking about the one with whom they had intercourse. It happens all the time.

Another example is the man who abuses or cheats on his wife. The wife will tolerate it, not able to separate and free herself of this abuse. Sometimes she becomes strong enough to separate for awhile, but she keeps going back with him time after time, even though it keeps hurting more and more. People will tolerate almost anything because of soul ties.

Divorce takes its toll as well. When a couple has been married and then gets a divorce, there is generally a strong, emotional tearing, usually affecting one partner worse than the other. Hurt turns to anger, then to resentment and bitterness. Sometimes one or more of these emotions can lead to downright ugly or violent behavior, and these emotions can grip a person for years unless the soul tie is broken. If there are children involved, they are often caught in the middle of all these emotions and can end up suffering the most.

The strength of the soul tie usually corresponds to the length of time involved in the relationship, but not always. Even a one-night stand can result in a soul tie. Many men develop strong soul ties to prostitutes.

Temptation, in and of itself, is not sin. However, when we act on the temptation, we sin against God.

As long as we say no to Satan's ploys, we are living in obedience to God. Romans 6:12 says, "Therefore do not let sin reign in your mortal body, that you should obey it in its lusts." Be sure your faith is firmly placed in the Lord, and He will rescue you. Resisting the enemy in your own power only leads to disappointment, frustrations and defeat. Galatians 5:16 says, "Walk in the Spirit, and you shall not fulfill the lust of the flesh." Only through the power of the Holy Spirit can we resist the enemy.

If you are presently involved, or have been involved in the past, in a soul-tie situation, and you want to get out from under that stronghold, here's what you must do through the power of the Holy Spirit:

1. You must first stop what you are doing to maintain the soul tie.
2. You must ask for forgiveness for the past or present conduct.
3. You must use the Word of God and ask "in Jesus' Name" that your spirits be loosed from one another (you and the other person), according to Matthew 18:18, "Assuredly, I say to you, whatever you bind on earth will be bound in heaven, and whatever you loose on earth will be loosed in heaven."
4. You must tell your spirit to forget the union(s).
5. You must tell your heart to tell your mind to release responsibility for the other person.
6. You must tell your emotions to "let go and forget."

By the power of the Holy Spirit, you will be set free from the emotional bondage of a "soul tie." God will heal you, comfort you and protect you. He is waiting to bless you.

Chapter Eighteen

Emotional Bondage

S HUMAN BEINGS, WE HAVE EMOTIONS—MANY OF them—and many books have been written about them. God intended for us to use them in a positive way to promote unity and good fellowship with our family and friends and to give us an inner sense of security, fulfillment and peacefulness. God has given us love, the greatest emotion of all, which has the ability to cover a multitude of sins. His love for us is so great it's unconditional. But have you ever noticed how quickly your love can turn to hate, your joy to sadness, and your peacefulness to strife? And how your family and closest friends seem to be able to hurt you the most?

Our soul consists of our mind, our emotions and our will.

Satan works on our minds and plays on our emotions. If he is successful, our emotions control us rather than the other way around. Anytime we are fearful, jealous, angry, haughty or feeling sorry for ourselves and these feelings do not dissipate quickly, we open the door for Satan to operate unhindered. Our emotions can cause us to get stuck in deception—with false mind sets, distorted viewpoints and warped attitudes. If we hang on to these mind sets, viewpoints and attitudes, we are headed for trouble. Our soul wants to control our actions via the flesh.

What makes you glad, sad or mad reveals the condition of your soul.

Do you get offended? Nowhere in the Bible does it show where Jesus, in spite of all the ridicule and persecution He received, "took anything personally." He simply did not get offended or indignant about what anyone said or did (other than when He had righteous indignation and became angry with the moneychangers in the temple). If He'd had a vindictive attitude toward His enemies, He would have been seeking revenge constantly because He certainly had many enemies. If we as Christians are to be more like Him, we must learn to control our negative emotions.

If we share our emotions with others when we are upset, it is easy to get even more upset. If they agree with us and their emotions get caught up with ours, that will fuel the fire. Pretty soon a spark of jealousy can become a jealous rage, or a spark of anger can become vindictiveness. If they disagree with us, we might get angry with them because of what we perceive as their lack of understanding, or try to argue our point of view and become even more frustrated. We might end up angrier at that other person than we were about the situation that caused us to be upset in the first place! That's why it's not usually a good idea to share our negative emotions with others.

I believe chapter 10 makes it clear how powerful our words are. If we mix anger in with our words, it can bring devastating results. Even Moses, one of the greatest men of all time, suffered the consequences of anger and frustration. The end result was that he was not allowed to lead the Israelites into the Promised Land!

Instead of sharing our emotions with others when we are upset, the Bible tells us in 1 Peter 5:7 to cast all our cares upon the Lord because He cares for us. We are not told to "unload" or "dump" on another person.

Galatians 6:5 says, "For each one shall bear his own load." Learning to bear your own load, however, is more difficult if you grew up in a dysfunctional home. Unfortunately, if you grew up in a home where your parents were emotionally unhealthy, you are much more likely to fall into the same emotional traps as they did. The good news is you do not have to stay there! No matter what your background, no matter what your history, no matter what your obstacles are, God can turn any situation or circumstance around if you diligently seek Him.

When our emotions get in the way, it can cause us to be alienated from family or friends. It can cause us to lose our spouses, our jobs, have a nervous breakdown or become severely depressed. It can cause all sorts of pain, wrong decisions and regrets. It can keep us living in the past or the future instead of the present. It can cause us to withdraw into our own little shell. It can produce stress and devastating physical illnesses.

Today, more and more people are going to therapists and taking antidepressants to try to heal the scars and break the bonds of emotional baggage. I'm not suggesting that having therapy or taking antidepressants is wrong, but only through Jesus Christ can we be free from the hurts and scars that each of us may have accumulated in the past or from the hurts we have yet to experience in the future. Only as each of us realizes who we are in Jesus Christ will we be able to let go of our emotional bondage.

This bondage I'm talking about can be a lot of different things. It may be hurt, fear, disappointment, discouragement, anger, self-centeredness, pride, selfishness, jealousy or envy. It could be guilt, shame, anxiety, worry, resentment, bitterness, depression, loneliness or unforgiveness. If you are caught up in one or more of these emotional traps, you may have an utter feeling of hopelessness. If any combination of these emotions is keeping you hostage, then that has probably become your greatest weakness.

Satan knows our weaknesses, and it is usually in our weakest state and at our weakest point that he attacks. In Luke 4:3–13, we see where Satan attacked Jesus in His weakest state when He had been fasting for forty days and forty nights in the wilderness. Three times Satan tempted Jesus, and Jesus resisted each time. Then in verse 13 we read: "Now when the devil had ended every temptation, he departed from Him until an opportune time." That tells me that even though we may deal with these emotional strongholds, the devil may still try to use them against us at a later, more opportune time—maybe at the next weak moment.

Even though you may know what emotions get in your way and you may know what needs to be done about them, you cannot do it through your own power. The Lord said to the apostle Paul, "My grace is sufficient for you, for My strength is made perfect in weakness" (2 Cor. 12:9). Only through the power of God's love and the power of the Holy Spirit can we be changed. Each of these emotional weaknesses must be dealt with in order to experience true freedom and victory.

When you were saved, your spirit was reborn, or born again. But until your soul (mind, will and emotions) and your body (flesh) come into agreement with your reborn spirit, there's going to be inner conflict. Feeding on the Word of God will produce a transformation of the mind. Set your mind on the things above. Meditate on God's Word until your thoughts are in complete agreement with His. Eventually, your emotions will yield, and your life won't be run on emotion. The body will follow—it will do whatever you tell it to do.

Agreement with God produces a life of complete integrity.

Your thoughts, your words and your actions will all match up with each other and with God's Word.

Once you are able to do that, your choices and actions will not be made based on emotion (or wrong mind-sets) but on reality, objectivity and a strong sense of who you are in Christ. Your self-esteem will be balanced, perfectly centered. You won't have an over-inflated sense of self worth (a big ego), nor will you have an under-inflated sense of self worth, constantly beating up on yourself. You won't be wallowing in self-pity, shame or guilt, or blaming someone else for all your problems. Instead, you will have true humility, which consists of thankfulness, generosity, kindness and full assurance that you are everything in

Christ and nothing without Him.

If you have a heavy spirit, a perpetual frown and a negative attitude, you shouldn't wonder why your unsaved family and friends don't want what you have. The joy of the Lord should be your strength, according to Nehemiah 8:10. Could it be the joy of the Lord is missing because of the emotional bondage of hurt, anger, pride, fear or envy? This bondage can rob you of your joy, your faith and your effectiveness as a Christian and can hinder your prayers. Satan knows that, and that is why he works so hard to use these emotions against us.

I believe when a person has complete deliverance from emotional bondage, that person can and will become more Christ-like in every way. I believe emotions are very much linked to addictions of alcohol, drugs, gambling, sex, food and even work-aholic behavior. I also believe they are linked to the obsessive-compulsive behavior of trying to control or rescue others; the need to be liked and get approval from others, and the entrapments of sexual sins, to name a few.

When you gain complete victory and have true freedom from emotional bondage, you may still experience some hurt and emotional pain, but you will not be *crushed* under the trials, tribulations and persecutions of life. Instead, as it says in Philippians 4:7, "the peace of God, which surpasses all understanding, will guard your hearts and minds through Christ Jesus."

Chapter Nineteen

Renewing Your Mind

E HAVE COVERED A GREAT DEAL OF MATERIAL dealing with a variety of spiritual strongholds, and it is up to you to apply the Word of God and use the tools available to you as a born-again believer. You do not have to live under or accept the bondage of the enemy in your life. When Jesus died on Calvary, He not only died for your sins, He died so that you could be an "overcomer." Jesus became the curse, so that you might be blessed.

You can and must use the power of the cross (which was the shedding of His blood) and reverse the curse. The blood of Jesus has the power to reverse the curse!

You must apply (plead) the blood over yourself or over your circumstances for it to be effective. You and I have the covenant (promise) of His blood to cleanse us from all sin through the sacrifice of

Christ. First John 1:7 makes it clear, "But if we walk in the light as He is in the light, we have fellowship with one another, and the blood of Jesus Christ His Son cleanses us from all sin."

The applying, or "pleading," of the blood of Jesus Christ was an accepted revelation of the Spirit in the early days of the Pentecostal outpouring. But, like many other divine revelations, it has been somewhat lost to man's organizational self-centeredness. When the blood is used, it brings effective, astounding results. The blood of Christ is a mighty weapon of spiritual warfare, holding the secret to a life of miracles and freedom.

Once you have reversed the curse or pulled down the stronghold in your family, business, health or any other area of your life, then you should release upon yourself and family a *powerful blessing*. You and I have authority—believer's authority—and God has given us the responsibility to use it. If you don't exercise your authority, it is useless! Ephesians 1:22 reads, "And He put all things under His feet and gave Him to be head over all things to the Church." We are the organic body of Christ here on earth. We are the feet!

The Bible says we are kings and priests: "But you are a chosen generation, a royal priesthood, a holy nation, His own special people, that you may proclaim the praises of Him who called you out of darkness into His marvelous light" (1 Pet. 2:9). In Revelation 5:10, we read, "And have made us kings and priests to our God." We, as believers, are kings and priests with spiritual responsibilities. God has given us the authority to speak blessings over our family, ourselves, our jobs, our ministries, our health and our finances—every single aspect of our lives. It's time we started using our rightful authority as Christians!

Praise precedes victory. We need to start praising God right now for the victory. Thank Him for making you victorious. Proclaim it and claim it! The Scriptures teach us that as a man thinks in his heart, so he is (Prov. 23:7). You cannot think negatively and believe positively, and you cannot believe negatively and live positively. The following scriptures emphasize the importance of our thought processes:

> Trust in the Lord with all your heart, and *lean not on your own understanding.*
>
> —PROVERBS 3:5, EMPHASIS ADDED

> That you put off, concerning your former conduct, the old man which grows corrupt according to the deceitful lusts, and be *renewed in the spirit of your mind,* and that you put on the new man which was created according to God, in true righteousness and holiness.
>
> —EPHESIANS 4:22–24, EMPHASIS ADDED

> For though we walk in the flesh, we do not war according to the flesh. For the weapons of our warfare are not carnal but mighty in God for pulling down strongholds, casting down arguments and every high thing that exalts itself against the knowledge of God, *bringing every thought into captivity* to the obedience of Christ.
>
> —2 CORINTHIANS 10:3–5, EMPHASIS ADDED

God's Word is a "power tool," as we see in Hebrews 4:12:

> For the word of God is living and powerful, and sharper than any two-edged sword, piercing

even to the division of soul and spirit, and of joints and marrow, and is a discerner of the thoughts and intents of the heart.

This "power tool," the Word of God, should be used against the devil and against curses. On every single occasion where Jesus was tempted by the devil, Jesus used the Word of God to defend Himself. He said, "It is written . . ." No other instruction on the face of the earth has the power to set us free like the inspired Word of God. We have the authority given to us as born-again believers, we have the blood that was shed to cover us, we have the Word of God, which covers every situation and circumstance, and, lastly, we have the name of Jesus, which brings terror to the enemy's camp.

If you believe there are strongholds in your life or a generational curse in your family and you want change, *you have to reverse the roles.* Satan needs to hear from you that he is no longer in charge. Whether he came in with your permission or without your permission, it doesn't matter. He will not leave willfully. Ecclesiastes 8:8 says, "And wickedness will not deliver those who are given to it." You will have to do your part to reverse the circumstances in your life. The more you obey God, the less permission you give Satan to operate in your life.

THE CHOICE IS YOURS

GOD IS THE AUTHOR AND FINISHER OF OUR FAITH. HE IS THE Alpha and the Omega, the beginning and the end. He started it all; He will finish it all. Everything in between is up to us based on the choices we make. The choice of whether we experience life or death, blessings or curses, is up to us. It has been this way since creation.

God has promised to "give of the fountain of the water of life freely to him who thirsts" (Rev. 21:6). He also tells us in Revelation 21:7–8:

> He who overcomes shall inherit all things, and I will be his God and he shall be My son. But the cowardly, unbelieving, abominable, murderers, sexually immoral, sorcerers, idolaters, and all liars shall have their part in the lake which burns with fire and brimstone, which is the second death.

When Jesus died on the cross, He not only provided for our eternal salvation, but He also gave us the ability and power to overcome "the flesh, the devil, and all the powers of darkness." He also came so that we could have life and have it more abundantly—in other words, so we could be blessed in every area of our lives. God did not say we would never have anything to wrestle with, but He did not intend for us to live weak, powerless and frustrated lives as Christians. He wants us to live in freedom, not bondage; in faith, not fear; in victory, not defeat.

A BLESSING IS YOURS TO RECEIVE

A. We must take action. To be free from strongholds, they must be renounced and broken— each and every one!

B. The Holy Spirit will reveal hidden conditions.

   1. Speak into that condition.

   2. Use your authority to bind and loose.

     a) To bind means to tie up (Satan) or to confine something—even words.

     b) To loose means to loose a blessing or to loose a person or thing from bondage.

C. Identify the root cause of your stronghold or curse. Name the spirit behind it—then bind it!

1. Be completely honest.

2. You must not be in denial.

3. Confess all known sin. (Ask the Holy Spirit to reveal any unknown sins.) There must be true repentance. Don't just go through the motions—God knows the difference. God will not be mocked—He knows your heart. If you are not serious about your repentance, don't expect to have victory. True repentance means a change in attitude and behavior.

4. Renounce any involvement with any area we are going to discuss as strongholds in the pages to follow.

5. Ask for forgiveness for anything you may have done that transgresses the commandments of God. Receive God's forgiveness, forgive yourself and then forgive others who may have wronged you.

D. Bless the Lord, bless your family and bless yourself. Bless those who curse you and pray for those who spitefully use you and persecute you, according to Matthew 5:44. Ask that blessings that have been withheld from you be loosed over you and your family. Bless and do not curse.

If you still have not asked Jesus to come into your life, turn back to the end of chapter 6 and do it now!

Chapter Twenty

Identify the Strongholds

MAJOR KEY FOR VICTORY IN THE PULLING DOWN OF strongholds in our lives is for us to identify if we are held captive by any.

SYMPTOMS OF A STRONGHOLD

- Any persistent act of disobedience or sin habit that is uncontrollable
- Uncontrolled behavior, i.e. language, anger and temper, violence
- Depression, mental breakdown, confusion or fear
- Repeated failure, never able to fully succeed
- Poverty cycle, never seeming to have enough
- Sickness and disease that "runs in the family" that doesn't respond to prayer or medical treatment
- Uncontrolled desire, lust, perversion, which

results in sexual sins, such as pornography, adultery, fornication, incest, etc.

- Addictions to drugs, alcohol, gambling, food or other things
- Breakdown in family relations—divorce

SELF-EXAMINATION

- Are you still struggling with the same problem after much prayer and true repentance?
- Are you living in personal, known, unconfessed sin?
- Have you had chronic physical problems all your life?
- Has illicit and unnatural sex been manifested either in you or your family line?
- Are you, or have you in the past, spoken bitter, hateful words over your own children or other family members?
- Have you or any of your ancestors been involved in the occult—fortunetelling, psychics, astrology, Ouija boards, etc?
- Do you recall hateful, bitter words being spoken over you by your parents or by another authority figure?

If you answered yes to any of the above questions, the following pages may help you identify the areas of strongholds or curses in your own life. Each stronghold is listed, as well as many of the manifestations of that particular stronghold, which should make it easier for you to identify and then renounce.

IDENTIFICATION PAGE—Renounce

STRONGHOLD OF DIVINATION
(Linked with familiar spirits)

MANIFESTATIONS

- ❏ Fortuneteller
- ❏ Psychic
- ❏ Sorcerer
- ❏ Mind science
- ❏ Witch or warlock
- ❏ Astrology
- ❏ Horoscopes
- ❏ Tarot cards
- ❏ Ouija board
- ❏ Black or white magic
- ❏ Voodoo
- ❏ Mediums
- ❏ Magic charms
- ❏ Blood pacts

- ❏ Water witching—divination
- ❏ Star gazing—zodiac
- ❏ Rebellion
- ❏ Spiritualist
- ❏ Clairvoyant
- ❏ Astral projection
- ❏ Speaking in a trance
- ❏ Materialization
- ❏ Belief in ghosts
- ❏ Table lifting
- ❏ Palm reader
- ❏ Amateur hypnosis
- ❏ Mental suggestions
- ❏ Other

IDENTIFICATION PAGE—Renounce

STRONGHOLD OF ANTICHRIST
(Linked with stronghold of seducing spirits)

MANIFESTATIONS

- ❑ Humanism
- ❑ Anti-Christian
- ❑ Lawlessness
- ❑ Antichrist (against Christ and His teachings)
- ❑ Teachers of heresies
- ❑ Atheist
- ❑ Agnostic
- ❑ Worldly speech and actions
- ❑ Suppresses ministries
- ❑ Denies atonement
- ❑ Denies deity of Christ
- ❑ Deceiver

"And every spirit that does not confess that Jesus Christ has come in the flesh is not of God. And this is the spirit of the Antichrist, which you have heard was coming, and is now already in the world."—1 John 4:3

MANIFESTATIONS

- ❑ Filthy mind
- ❑ Sexual perversions
- ❑ Doctrinal error (twisting the Word)
- ❑ Evil actions
- ❑ Pornography
- ❑ Child abuse
- ❑ Prostitution
- ❑ Homosexual or lesbian
- ❑ Bisexual
- ❑ Molestation
- ❑ Incest
- ❑ Rape
- ❑ Transvestite
- ❑ Seared conscience
- ❑ Obsessive masturbation or sex
- ❑ Contentious
- ❑ Foolish
- ❑ Lust
- ❑ Vanity
- ❑ Frigid
- ❑ Effeminate spirit: having feminine qualities
- ❑ Pedophilia: sexual perversion in which children are the preferred sexual object
- ❑ Pederast: lover of boys
- ❑ Catamite: a boy kept by a pederast
- ❑ Sodomy: sexual intercourse with a member of the same sex or with an animal

IDENTIFICATION PAGE—Renounce
Stronghold of Error

MANIFESTATIONS

- ❏ Defensive/argumentative
- ❏ New Age movement
- ❏ Having a form of godliness (but denying its power)
- ❏ Error in doctrine
- ❏ Confusion
- ❏ False doctrines
- ❏ Unsubmissive
- ❏ Giving false prophecy
- ❏ Moving in the gifts of the Spirit in error
- ❏ Contentious
- ❏ Doubts and fears

"We are of God. He who knows God hears us; he who is not of God does not hear us. By this we know the spirit of truth and the spirit of error."—1 John 4:6

IDENTIFICATION PAGE—Renounce

Stronghold of Whoredoms

(Linked with divination, error, perverse and familiar spirits)

MANIFESTATIONS

- ❏ Unfaithfulness / adultery
- ❏ Worldliness
- ❏ Prostitution
- ❏ Fornication
- ❏ Self-centeredness
- ❏ Obsession with sex
- ❏ Lust
- ❏ Chronic dissatisfaction
- ❏ Idolatry—love of money
- ❏ Soul tie (emotional bondage as a result of sexual involvement)
- ❏ Sexual spirits: incubus, succubus

  Incubus: an evil spirit that can have sexual intercourse with women in their sleep

  Succubus: an evil spirit that has sexual intercourse with men in their sleep

IDENTIFICATION PAGE—Renounce
STRONGHOLD OF JEALOUSY

MANIFESTATIONS

- ❑ **Murderous**
- ❑ **Jealous**
- ❑ **Cruel or spiteful**
- ❑ **Critical**
- ❑ **Angry (may be suppressed anger)**
- ❑ **Causes division, strife**
- ❑ **Envious and covetous**
- ❑ **Very competitive**
- ❑ **Selfish**
- ❑ **Hateful**
- ❑ **Violent rage**
- ❑ **Vindictive**
- ❑ **Bitter**

"Now Cain talked with Abel his brother; and it came to pass, when they were in the field, that Cain rose up against Abel his brother and killed him."—Genesis 4:8

MANIFESTATIONS

❑ Fear of rejection
❑ Fear of being alone
❑ Fear of intimidation
❑ Fear of the dark
❑ Fear of death or dying
❑ Fear of not getting approval of others
❑ Fear of not being liked or loved by others
❑ Fear of persecution
❑ Fear of failure or making mistakes
❑ Fear of the unknown
❑ Dread (evil forebodings)
❑ Fear of saying no
❑ Fear of change

❑ Fear of confrontation
❑ Fear of embarrassment
❑ Panic attack
❑ Feeling not good enough
❑ Fear of crime or violence
❑ Fear of man
❑ Stress—Anxiety—Worry
❑ Withdrawal
❑ Torment
❑ Terror
❑ Nightmares
❑ Insomnia
❑ Fear of what others will think or say
❑ Lack of assertiveness
❑ Paranoia

MANIFESTATIONS

- ❏ Compulsive liar
- ❏ Breaks agreements or contracts
- ❏ Slanderous—makes false accusations
- ❏ Flatterer
- ❏ Gossips
- ❏ Exaggerates
- ❏ Perpetuates superstitions
- ❏ Can no longer recognize the truth
- ❏ False sense of responsibility or burden
- ❏ Falsely prophesies

MANIFESTATIONS

- ❑ Physical problem medical doctors cannot diagnose
- ❑ Tried everything and symptoms don't go away
- ❑ Problems seems to travel from one part of the body to another
- ❑ Physical malady that usually "runs in the family," such as, but not limited to:
  - Cancer
  - Arthritis
  - Allergies
  - Asthma
  - Diabetes
- ❑ Has fear of infirmities and confesses it
- ❑ Chronic health problems throughout one's life
- ❑ Often diagnosed as hypochondriac
- ❑ Lingering disorders
- ❑ Impotent—frail—lame—weak
- ❑ Bent body—spine
- ❑ Fever

IDENTIFICATION PAGE—Renounce

STRONGHOLD OF DEATH
(Plans of the enemy against one's life)

MANIFESTATIONS

❑ **Accident prone**
❑ **Involved in random acts of violence**
❑ **Fatal diseases**
❑ **Excessive clumsiness**
❑ **Excessive fighting**
❑ **Suicidal attempts**

IDENTIFICATION PAGE—Renounce
ASSOCIATION WITH CULT(S)

MANIFESTATIONS

❏ Christian Science
❏ Transcendental meditation
❏ Scientology
❏ Silva mind control
❏ Unification church
❏ Church of the Living Word
❏ Mormonism
❏ Jehovah's Witnesses
❏ Children of God
❏ Masons
❏ New Age
❏ Buhaism
❏ Zen Buddhism
❏ Channeling
❏ Yoga
❏ Unity
❏ Other (allow the Holy Spirit
  to show you)

❏ The Way
❏ Hinduism
❏ Father Divine
❏ Roy Masters
❏ Islam or those who
  claim Islam
❏ Black Islam
❏ Science of Mind
❏ Hare Krishna
❏ Rosicrucian
❏ Any supremacist or
  separatist group
  (of any race)
❏ Divine Science
❏ EST
❏ Religious Science

A cult is a religion (or movement) regarded as unorthodox or spurious. (Spurious means "outwardly similar to something without having its genuine qualities; false; of a deceitful nature or quality.") Seducing spirits are the evil forces behind cults.

IDENTIFICATION PAGE—Renounce
STRONGHOLD OF PRACTICING IDOLATRY

MANIFESTATIONS

Do you worship:
- ❏ A religion*
- ❏ People—living or dead, Buddha, etc.
- ❏ Figures or statues
- ❏ Even the cross, relics, etc.
- ❏ Spouse
- ❏ Job
- ❏ Automobiles
- ❏ Boats
- ❏ Money
- ❏ Material things—(Debt may be the result and may be the curse.)
- ❏ Other

*Worshipping a religion indicates a religious spirit. God desires that we have a relationship with Him—not just go through a ritual form of worship.

Does greed, pride or covetousness get in your way? Any desire of the heart can be an idol—anything we worship and esteem higher than we do God. We can be deceived by the desires of our heart—God will allow it to take on a voice of deception.

IDENTIFICATION PAGE—Renounce

STRONGHOLD OF HAUGHTINESS (PRIDE)
(Linked with stronghold of lying)

MANIFESTATIONS

- ❑ Pride
- ❑ Indignation
- ❑ Conceit
- ❑ Superiority feelings
- ❑ Arrogant or smug
- ❑ Attention seeker— "look at me" attitude
- ❑ Boastful or bragger
- ❑ Idleness
- ❑ Domineering
- ❑ Manipulative
- ❑ Impatient
- ❑ Self-righteous
- ❑ Rebellious—obstinate
- ❑ Gossip (especially malicious)
- ❑ Big ego
- ❑ Needs to be right all the time
- ❑ Contentious—full of strife
- ❑ Interrupts others
- ❑ Dictatorial—controlling
- ❑ Scornful
- ❑ Self-deception
- ❑ Self-willed
- ❑ Self-centered

IDENTIFICATION PAGE—Renounce
STRONGHOLD OF HEAVINESS
(Linked with stronghold of infirmity)

MANIFESTATIONS

- ❑ Feeling of gloom
- ❑ Low self-esteem
- ❑ Excessive grief or sorrow
- ❑ Insomnia or excessive sleeping
- ❑ Depression
- ❑ Hopelessness (contemplating suicide)
- ❑ Has "hurts" that won't go away
- ❑ Self-pity
- ❑ Fatigue
- ❑ Passive
- ❑ Emotions suppressed
- ❑ Gluttony
- ❑ Loneliness
- ❑ Negative outlook
- ❑ Broken heart

IDENTIFICATION PAGE—Renounce

STRONGHOLD OF DEAF AND DUMB SPIRIT
(See Mark 9:17–29.)

MANIFESTATIONS

- ❏ Epilepsy (Matt. 17:15)
- ❏ Self-mutilation (Mark 5:5)
- ❏ Autism
- ❏ Mental illness
- ❏ Blind/mute (Matt. 12:22)
- ❏ Hearing voices
- ❏ Palsy
- ❏ Mute—unable to speak (Matt. 9:32–33)
- ❏ Seizures/convulsions (Mark 9:18,20,26)
- ❏ Attempts to end one's life (Mark 9:22)

IDENTIFICATION PAGE—Renounce
STRONGHOLD OF EMOTIONAL BONDAGE

MANIFESTATIONS

- ❑ **Fear**
- ❑ **Pride**
- ❑ **Jealousy**
- ❑ **Anger**
  - • **Spiteful—vindictive—seeking revenge**
  - • **Hurt**
  - • **Bitter**
  - • **Destructive**
- ❑ **Heaviness**
- ❑ **Hatred**
- ❑ **Unforgiving**
- ❑ **Complacency (apathetic, passive, lack of commitment or follow through)**
- ❑ **Discouragement**
- ❑ **Discontent**
- ❑ **Burden of guilt or shame**
- ❑ **Resentment or blame**
- ❑ **No desire to live—suicidal**
- ❑ **Soul tie (see end of chapter 17 to get release from this bondage.)**

MANIFESTATIONS

- ❏ Stealing
- ❏ Violence
- ❏ Profanity
- ❏ Murder—including abortion
- ❏ Rebellion
- ❏ Doubt and/or unbelief
- ❏ Confusion
- ❏ Greed
- ❏ Religious spirit
  (See "Idolatrous Practices")
- ❏ Poverty or lack
  - Stubborn
    (refuses correction)
  - Negative attitude
    toward authority
  - Laziness
  - Procrastination
  - Argumentative
  - Disrespectful
- ❏ Addictions
  - Illegal drugs
  - Prescription drugs
  - Alcohol
  - Smoking (nicotine)
  - Gambling
  - Food (see eating disorder)
  - Job (workaholic)
- ❏ Obsessive compulsive behavior:
  - Shopping/
    over-spending/debt
  - Eating disorder
    Gluttony
    Anorexia
    Bulimia
  - Codependency
    Controlling or
    rescuing others
    Manipulative
    Blaming others
    False sense of
    responsibility
    Lying
    Burden of guilt/shame
    Over-reacting
    Taking things
    personally
- ❏ Other generational curse
  - Effect of negative words
- ❏ Any other hereditary problem (Ask the Holy Spirit to show you)

The Next Steps

When we are born again, we are supernaturally made a new creation as the Bible says in 2 Corinthians 5:17, "Therefore, if anyone is in Christ, he is a new creation; old things have passed away; behold, all things have become new."

We should not go on feelings but on what we know God's Word says. We don't have to feel anything—only know by faith, believe and receive.

Begin, confess and repent (speak aloud!)

1. Admit that other people have spoken negative, hurtful or damning words over you and released evil forces into your spirit and your life.
2. Forgive those who have done so. No forgiveness—no deliverance! Forgiveness and deliverance are connected.
3. Identify and name any and all curses from previous generations; reject and disown the sins of your ancestors.
4. Acknowledge and confess any known sin on your part. Ask God for forgiveness.
5. When we confess our sins, God forgives and forgets our sins supernaturally. So must we. Once we have been forgiven, we need to forgive ourselves and lay aside any feelings of guilt, shame or condemnation.

6. Renounce all strongholds in your life, one at a time, that you have identified using the lists on the previous pages.

7. You must bind the enemy of your life, and bind him from operating in your households. Bind the power of Satan to operate in your life and the lives of the young children in your household who are under the age of accountability.

8. Give back the curse and spoil his house by releasing a powerful blessing and declaring that God will keep you and your family.

9. Apply the name of Jesus and the blood of Jesus over yourself, your family and your circumstances. God will turn things around for you. Do not give up on God, and do not give in to the devil!

RENUNCIATION PRAYER #1 (Pray aloud!)

(For generational curses and all strongholds)

Dear heavenly Father,

As a child of God, purchased by the blood of the Lord Jesus Christ, I hereby now reject and disown all the sins of my ancestors; as one who has been delivered from the power of darkness and translated into the kingdom of God through His dear Son, Jesus.

I bind and cancel all demonic working that has been passed on to me from my ancestors. As one who has been crucified with Jesus Christ and raised to walk in newness of life, I bind and cancel every curse, or spell, that has been put on me, or any objects in my possession.

(Using the stronghold identification pages, name all the areas that the Holy Spirit has shown you, renouncing each stronghold in your life.)

I have struggled with _____ *(name the strong-hold)* _____, *but as of this moment, I renounce* _____ *(name the stronghold) and it will never again interfere in my life! I take charge and use my authority as a born-again believer!*

I announce to Satan and all his forces that Christ became a curse for me when He hung on the cross. As one who has been crucified and raised with Christ and now sits with Him in heavenly places, I reject every way in which Satan may try to claim ownership of me. I declare myself to be completely signed over and committed to the Lord Jesus Christ.

I bind and command every familiar spirit and every enemy of the Lord Jesus that is oppressing me to leave me and remain gone. I now ask You, Lord, to fill me with your Holy Spirit, and I submit my body and soul to You as an instrument of righteousness, a living sacrifice, that I may glorify You in every way. All this I do in the name and authority of the Lord Jesus Christ. Amen.

RENUNCIATION PRAYER #2 (PRAY ALOUD!)

(FOR ANY ADDICTION OR OBSESSIVE BEHAVIOR—
DRUGS, ALCOHOL, SMOKING, FOOD, GAMBLING, ETC.)

Dear heavenly Father,

You love me; You sent Jesus to set the captives free. The curse of my addiction to _____ *(name addiction)* _____ *is going to stop this very moment. Never again will I have this problem. I give this addiction to Jesus—"Jesus—set me free!" I am covered by Your name and by Your blood that cleanses me right now, and I am free by the blood, in the name of Jesus.*

As a born-again believer, I take charge and use my authority! Satan, you and your familiar evil spirits of obses-sion and addiction have heard my prayer right now. You've had your chance, but your power is broken—NOW! Never again will I be a slave to _____ *(name addiction)*

In Jesus' name, this curse is broken, this interference in my life is stopped right now. I am delivered!

I bind and command every familiar spirit and every enemy of the Lord Jesus Christ that is oppressing me to leave me and remain gone. I now ask You, Lord, to fill me with your Holy Spirit, and I submit my body and soul to you as an instrument of righteousness, a living sacrifice, that I may glorify you in every way. All this I do in the name and authority of the Lord Jesus Christ. Amen.

Once you have prayed about each and every stronghold or curse affecting your life, pray the powerful blessing found in Numbers 6:24–26 aloud over yourself and your household (insert the word "me" in place of "you" if you are praying by yourself).

"The Lord bless you and keep you; the Lord make His face shine upon you, and be gracious to you; the Lord lift up His countenance upon you, and give you peace."

Chapter Twenty One

Standing Firm in Your Deliverance

ELIVERANCE IS NOT A QUICK FIX; IT IS ONLY THE beginning. Each day you will need to walk the new walk. Each day you will choose whom you will serve, as the Word of God says in Joshua 24:15: "Choose for yourselves this day whom you will serve." Matthew 6:24 clearly says we cannot serve two masters. If we submit to God and resist the devil, he will flee from us (James 4:7). There is no doubt he will try to attack again, but we must stand firm in our deliverance and not be subject again to any yoke of bondage.

Every day we should arm ourselves with our defensive weapons, which are:

1. Putting on our spiritual armor.

Finally, my brethren, be strong in the Lord and in the power of His might. Put on the whole armor of God, that you may be able to stand against the wiles of the devil. For we do not wrestle against flesh and blood, but against principalities, against powers, against the rulers of the darkness of this age, against spiritual hosts of wickedness in the heavenly places. Therefore take up the whole armor of God, that you may be able to withstand in the evil day, and having done all, to stand. Stand therefore, having girded your waist with truth, having put on the breastplate of righteousness, and having shod your feet with the preparation of the gospel of peace; above all, taking the shield of faith with which you will be able to quench all the fiery darts of the wicked one. And take the helmet of salvation, and the sword of the Spirit, which is the word of God; praying always with all prayer and supplication in the Spirit, being watchful to this end with all perseverance and supplication for all the saints.

—EPHESIANS 6:10–18

2. Renewing our minds through God's Word.

I beseech you therefore, brethren, by the mercies of God, that you present your bodies a living sacrifice, holy, acceptable to God, which is your reasonable service. And do not be conformed to this world, but be transformed by the renewing of your mind, that you may prove what is that good and acceptable and perfect will of God.

—ROMANS 12:1–2

3. Submitting ourselves to God and drawing near to Him.

Therefore submit to God. Resist the devil and he will flee from you. Draw near to God and He will draw near to you.

—JAMES 4:7–8

It doesn't do a lot of good to resist the devil if you

are not first submitting your life to God. He will just step up his attack! If there is an area of your life you haven't submitted yet, that's probably the area the devil will target. We must learn to identify the strategies of the devil, identify when we are under an attack, and learn how to use our offensive weapons. Our offensive weapons are:

1. Prayer, praise and a verbal (outward) confession of faith.
Speak it out loud.

- "Pray without ceasing" (1 Thess. 5:17). We should have a prayerful attitude at all times.
- "The effective, fervent prayer of a righteous man avails much" (James 5:16).
- "Let them praise the name of the Lord, for His name alone is exalted; His glory is above the earth and heaven" (Ps. 148:13).
- "He who is in you is greater than he who is in the world" (1 John 4:4).

2. The Word of God

For the word of God is living and powerful, and sharper than any two-edged sword, piercing even to the division of soul and spirit, and of joints and marrow, and is a discerner of the thoughts and intents of the heart.

—HEBREWS 4:12

3. The Holy Spirit

Likewise the Spirit also helps in our weaknesses. For we do not know what we should pray for as we ought, but the Spirit Himself makes intercession for us with groanings which cannot be uttered. Now He who searches the hearts knows what the mind of the Spirit is, because

He makes intercession for the saints according to the will of God. And we know that all things work together for good to those who love God, to those who are called according to His purpose.

—ROMANS 8:26–28

4. The name of Jesus

And these signs will follow those who believe: In My name they will cast out demons; they will speak with new tongues . . . they will lay hands on the sick, and they will recover.

—MARK 16:17–18

5. The blood of Jesus

And they overcame him [Satan] by the blood of the Lamb [Jesus] and by the word of their testimony.

—REVELATION 12:11

With these weapons, we have the power and authority to defeat the devil every single day. With these weapons, we can and will be victorious.

"WALKING THE WALK" OF DELIVERANCE

EVIL SPIRITS WILL TRY TO RETURN. MATTHEW 12:43–45 SAYS:

When a defiling evil spirit is expelled from someone, it drifts along through the desert looking for an oasis, some unsuspecting soul it can bedevil. When it doesn't find anyone, it says, "I'll go back to my old haunt." On return it finds the person spotlessly clean, but vacant. It then runs out and rounds up seven other spirits more evil than itself and they all move in, whooping it up. That person ends up far worse off than if he'd never gotten cleaned up in the first place.

—THE MESSAGE

Our flesh has been trained to flow with the world's system—downstream. That's the natural flow of things, the easy way, the path of least resistance. Going against the grain of the world is difficult. It takes courage, discipline, determination and perseverance. Prayer strengthens our resolve. Matthew 26:41 says, "Watch and pray, lest you enter into temptation. The spirit indeed is willing, but the flesh is weak."

After Satan tempted Jesus, Scriptures say he planned to renew his attacks at "an opportune time" (Luke 4:13). Satan knows our weaknesses, and he will renew his attacks at our weakest moments! It might be when you are sick, physically exhausted, under a lot of stress at work or at home or something of that nature.

Don't get too busy for God!

Just being aware of the devil's strategy will help a lot. If he can control your thoughts, he will eventually control your actions!

Galatians 5:1 says, "Stand fast in the liberty by which Christ has made us free, and do not be entangled again with a yoke of bondage." If you practice the following, you will find your weakest moments are few and far between. You will find yourself being transformed from "glory to glory" and from "faith to faith." You will find yourself "growing up" in Christ, and it should be nearly impossible for you to be "entangled again with a yoke of bondage."

1. Read and study the Bible daily and allow your mind to be renewed and transformed by it. Live by it!
2. Confess the Scriptures aloud, especially those that apply to the circumstances in your life.

3. Make Jesus Christ number one in your life. Submit to Him and allow Him to lead and guide you and help you make the right decisions.
4. Avoid those people who were and are a bad influence. Choose Christian friends.
5. Prayer is vital—do not neglect it. It does not have to be done in a certain way, at a certain time, or in a certain place, but it should be aloud to be most effective. Also, pray in the Spirit.
6. Get grounded in a full gospel, Spirit-filled church where you will be nurtured, where you can grow spiritually and where you can serve the Lord. Seek His will for your life.
7. Practice praise and worship even when not in church.
8. Ask the Holy Spirit to fill you afresh every day.
9. Learn how to crucify the flesh and how to take authority over all demonic attacks.
10. Learn the strategies of the devil, and use your weapons of defense according to Ephesians 6:10–18, Romans 12:1–2 and James 4:7–8.
11. Be ready with your weapons of offense—1) prayer, praise, and a positive confession of faith, 2) the Word of God, 3) the Holy Spirit, 4) the name of Jesus, and 5) the blood of Jesus.
12. Submit to one another in love and humility, and guard against the buildup of resentments and a root of bitterness.
13. Don't dwell on your past failures. Learn from your mistakes and move on. Confess your sins immediately and remember God can turn a mistake into a miracle.

14. Have a thankful heart always, and a thankful mouth.
15. Give God the glory for every success and victory in your life. Say it to God, to yourself and to everyone around you. Share your testimony!

How to Protect Yourself From the Enemy

1. Plead/apply the blood of Jesus over yourself, your family and others daily.
2. Put on the whole armor of God each day according to Ephesians 6:10–18.
3. Bless the Lord; bless your family, yourself, health, job, automobile and finances. Curse the works of Satan—anything evil, including sickness, disease and poverty. God wants you healthy and prosperous.
4. Learn to recognize the creeping back of old habits and the old nature that were bound and removed from your life. To make sure an old habit doesn't come back, you may need to replace it with a new one.
5. Know that the enemy of your soul will not give up, and the mind is the battlefield. Remember, conviction comes from the Holy Spirit; condemnation comes from Satan. God wants to give you grace; Satan wants to give you disgrace.
6. The devil will try to make you believe all sorts of lies to steal your peace, your joy and your deliverance. He will twist and pervert the truth in every subtle way imaginable. Don't believe him!

7. Never again confess:
   - Defeat, or say "I can't."
   - Fear, doubt, unbelief or lack of faith
   - Poverty or lack
   - Weakness, sickness, worries or frustration
   - Lack of wisdom or good judgment
   - Bondage or condemnation

For in confessing these things you are giving Satan an opportunity to gain supremacy over your life in one area or another. Remember 1 John 4:4, "You are of God, little children, and have overcome them, because He who is in you is greater than he who is in the world."

8. Pray the following prayer aloud each and every day as a covering over you and your family:

Dear heavenly Father,

I pray this prayer in the power of the Holy Spirit. I thank You for all that You have done in my life and all that I know You are going to do. (Thank Him for specific blessings each day.)

I confess that I am healed and whole—physically, mentally, emotionally and spiritually. As your child, I stand on your Word that no weapon formed against me shall prosper (Is. 54:17). I put on the whole armor of God according to Ephesians 6:10–18.

I have a blood covenant with You, Father. Because of that covenant, I have authority over all ungodliness that may come against my family or myself. I bind and bring to no effect any and all curses that have been spoken against me or my family. I bind and render useless all spoken negative words directed at me or my family, whether they be witchcraft, psychic or soul force.

I bind and bring to no effect all demonic attacks against my family and myself, our minds, our bodies, our home, our automobiles, our finances and every area of our lives. I use my authority in Jesus' name to bind any fear spirits, hindering spirits, and deceiving spirits, including complacency, criticism, gossip, slander, jealousy, pride, envy, strife, hate and anger that may try to come against me.

Lord, I ask You to fill me afresh today with the Holy Spirit, to lead and guide me, giving me wisdom and discernment over all I do and say. As I walk in Your love, please let me be prosperous in all I set my hand to do.

I pray for opportunities to share the gospel and plant seeds. I pray for the wisdom to walk in Your will and to make the right choices. I call forth divine appointments and open doors of opportunity to share my testimony, and I will give You all the glory, honor and praise always!

I cover my family and myself with the protective power of the blood of Jesus. I ask the protection of Your holy angels to surround (our children, our grandchildren) and us in every area of our lives. I ask this prayer in the power and the precious name of Jesus, my Lord and Savior. Amen.

Note: If you are praying this prayer with your spouse each day, you may change the "I" to "we."

It is my hope and prayer that this book has shown you many of the ways that we, even as born-again Christians, open the door for the enemy. I don't believe Jesus is coming back for a church that is weak or fearful. I don't believe Jesus is coming back for a church that is full of doubt or unbelief. I believe you were saved to be an overcomer. God wants to bless you so you can be a blessing to others. As you stand firm in your deliverance by doing the things outlined in this chapter, your faith will become stronger and stronger, and I believe you will walk in victory as never before!

God loves you with a great and merciful love!
God bless you, and I bless you in the Name of Jesus!

Resources

Strong, James. *New Strong's Exhaustive Concordance of the Bible.* Nashville: Thomas Nelson Publishers, 1984.

Webster's New World Dictionary, second concise edition. New York: Simon & Schuster, 1982, 1979, 1977, 1975.

Merriam Webster's Collegiate Dictionary, tenth edition. Merriam-Webster, 1997.

If your life has been changed by this book,
please write and let us know in what way.
We look forward to hearing from you.
(Your prayer requests are welcome.)

To contact the author, write:

FREE INDEED MINISTRIES

P. O. Box 515066 • St. Louis, MO 63151–5066

OR

e-mail: PRallo@msn.com

For additional information, visit our website at:
www.freeindeedministries.org